Also by L. E. Hewitt

Life Between the Raindrops
My Wonderful Chaos
I Don't Have a Button for That
My Bucket List Has a Hole in It

Chasing the Silver Lining

L.E. HEWITT

SEABOARD PRESS
JAMES A. ROCK & COMPANY, PUBLISHERS

Chasing the Silver Lining by L. E. Hewitt

SEABOARD PRESS

is an imprint of JAMES A. ROCK & CO., PUBLISHERS

Chasing the Silver Lining copyright ©2015 by L.E. Hewitt

Special contents of this edition copyright ©2015 by Seaboard Press

All applicable copyrights and other rights reserved worldwide. No part of this publication may be reproduced, in any form or by any means, for any purpose, except as provided by the U.S. Copyright Law, without the express, written permission of the publisher.

Note: Product names, logos, brands, and other trademarks occurring or referred to within this work are the property of their respective trademark holders.

Address comments and inquiries to:
SEABOARD PRESS
1937 West Palmetto Street, #6
Florence, South Carolina 29501

E-mail:
jrock@rockpublishing.com   lrock@rockpublishing.com
Internet URL: www.rockpublishing.com

Trade Paperback ISBN: 978-1-59663-872-9

Printed in the United States of America

First Edition: 2015

Interested readers may wish to visit the author's website:
www.lehewitt.com

*This book
is dedicated to
mom*

*She always
sends me
in the
right direction
with
a hard nudge*

Contents

FuzzButt and the Others 1
How to get Things Done 4
College Bound 7
Falling into Fall 9
Evelyn's Basketballs 11
Being Unique 13
Paige 15
Single Parenting 17
What About Me? 19
Golden Years 21
Feeding the Tribe 23
My Special Day 25
Enjoy Today 27
Reflections 29
Voice to Text 31
Inside My Mind 33
My Wandering Mind 35
Expect the Unexpected 37
Wasting 39
Spooky 41
Freeloading Mutts 42
Losing to the Dogs 44
Troubles are a Comin' 46
Post Super Bowl Blues 48
No Respect 50
My Broken Heart 52
Dog Delivery 53
Never Settle 55
Women 56
Impatient 57
Tater Salad Taxes 58

Discovering Potential	60
Stop, Look, Listen	61
Swinger	63
Aging Gracefully	65
Understanding a Woman	67
Geese	69
Mechanics	72
Yard Sale Mania	73
Scheduling	75
Free Labor	77
Loving Life	78
Mowing and Blowing	80
Forward one day …	81
Petty Things	83
Live a Little	85
Keys	87
My Prescription	89
Where's My Beef?	91
The House That Built Me	93
Growth Spurt	96
Even More Yard Sale Mania	97
That's My Boy	100
Mean Old Mom	101
Spoiled Pets	103
Seasons	105
Cherry Juice	106
ME Day	108
Riding in Style	110
Grilled	112
Wisdom	114
Fee Me	116
Dad's Day	118
Mrs. P's	120

Diary of a Stroke	122
The Waiting	126
Prescribed Loafing	127
Un-Holiday	129
Introspection	131
Payday	132
My First New Car	134
The Fairest of the Fairs	136
Hairball	138
Old Dog	139
Al Ironed Out	141
Swim	143
Planning Project	145
Doctor Bill	147
Jello Blues	148
Mystery of Life	151
That's My Girl	153
Stories	154
Spoiled Plans	156
Gardens	157
Potty Procedures	159
A Charlie Brown World	161
The Stick Bug Theory	163
Hands From Heaven	167
My Helper	168
Take That, Sparky	170
Forms	172
Fire In the Hole	174
Sneeze	176
Smelling Dinner	177
Sharing My Knowledge	178
Diagnosing Myself	180
Pushing the Purse	182

Foreword

It has been a few long years since my previous writings to you. If you are a newcomer, welcome to my wonderfully strange world. If you are a returning reader, then I need to catch you up on a few things before we begin our new journey together. In these six or seven years, the kids have grown into college students. They have become responsible young adults. They are probably more responsible than I am, truth be known. Sally finally decided she had put up with enough of my shenanigans and moved on with her life without me. Wendy came along and spent some time in my world. We dated for several months, but in the end she decided that, as she put it, I was a great guy, just not her great guy. That's ok too, Life is unpredictable and while I believe I am a decent human being, I am far from flawless just like everybody else. So I do not blame anyone for the decisions they have made. I just keep smiling and moving forward.

I also had a health scare a few years back, a mild stroke. I went through some challenging times physically and emotionally, but in the end I feel it made me a better person. Being poked and prodded on a regular basis with an uncertain future made me learn to enjoy each moment of every day even more. It also gave me a different view on negativity. I no longer allow it in my life. I chose to take control of my life rather than allow my life to control me. I chose each day to smile more, laugh more and live more. Some odd things happened as a result. I turned off the television and tuned in to my life. I started saying exactly what I felt in a positive way. I started looking for opportunities to turn someone's negative attitude into a positive one and I was not afraid to openly embrace positive ideas in which I believe. I stopped worrying about what others might think and began to trust in my own judgment and follow my heart.

The stories in this book are another collection of humorous, uplifting and hopefully entertaining stories based on true events. I believe these things happen in everyone's lives. I think I just view the world differently. My goal with this book is to make you laugh out loud and cry at least once. If you snort your drink up your nose, then that is just a bonus. Most of all, I hope that my stories, both happy and sad, cause you to reflect upon the good memories of your own life and realize how blessed you truly are. So, now let's begin our next journey, *Chasing The Silver Lining*.

FuzzButt and the Others

We own four dogs and three cats. Well, I take that back … one dog is disguised in the body of a Seal Pointe Siamese cat. He acts more like a dog than some dogs do. He comes when you say his name. He follows you around. He has even learned tricks. He sits up or "sits pretty," as some people say, and Will and Elizabeth have taught him to turn off light switches. I do, however, have to give him credit for being part cat too. He will sneak in the kitchen and steal food off the table or the stove top after dinner is over if we are not careful. He was once even seen dragging a whole pork chop down the stairs. It was one of those butterflied chops and was nearly as big as he is. He was walking all spread eagle just to support the weight of the thing! I know what his plan was going to be. He was going to sneak downstairs, have a big pig-out feast, then get sick from eating too much and find one of my shoes into which to deposit the excess.

His name is FuzzButt. For reasons unknown to us, he steals ponytail holders and stashes them in a pile somewhere hidden. All the females in the house will be complaining about no ponytail holders and then one day we will find maybe 50 of them hidden under a bed or sofa or stuffed down inside a register vent. They are still perfectly fine to use aside from the dried cat slobber. I don't see why the girls complain about a little thing like that.

The "real" dogs are a whole 'nuther story. People are duped into believing that dogs are man's best friend. The truth is that man is a dog's best servant. We currently have three of them who each are in the 30 to 60 pound range. Living in suburbia, we have been trained to feed them and walk them and take them outside to the bathroom. We also bathe them and brush them and even go out and find their favorite food for them. None of the dogs has ever brought me something to eat. They have never even offered to share something good they were eating with me. When they go outside to the bathroom, they stand there all smug while I pick up their "presents" from the neighbor's yard. I guarantee you that if I did my business out there not a one of them would offer to do the same for me. Sally is the one that says this is what we are supposed to do. I grew up in the country and I really didn't watch to see where the dog did his business nor did I ever go over to the neighbor and complain that they needed to come retrieve their dog's droppings from my place. I have been told it is a civilized thing they do here in suburbia. I often feel like these dogs are more important than me. Matter of fact, I am going to test that theory. I think I will go over and poop in that crazy lady's yard across the street. Then I will come home and tell Sally what I have done and that she had better go over and bag it before the old bat starts complaining. Sally would do that for the retriever, surely she will do that for me!

I mean, let's be realistic here, the fruits of my labor pay for the home we share and the heat and air conditioning and a million other amenities in our dogs' lives. What do the dogs do while I am at work? They sleep on my bed, steal stuff out of the trash can, bark at the mailman, admire the view out the window, lay on the heat register ... all while I work hard. How do I know all of this? FuzzButt told me. Anyhow, he suggested that the dogs should get jobs to help support the family. So if you or someone you know needs your toes washed or your dinner plates pre-rinsed, or you have a stuffed animal that needs de-stuffed, just give me a call and I will send one of the dogs over to work for cheap.

How to get Things Done

I never get caught up. I always have more to do than I can ever get done. Today is a Sunday where I have nowhere that I have to be, so this is a day to try to get some of those things done I have been meaning to get done. First thing I need to do is to make a list of all the stuff that needs done around here. That way I can set my priorities and make a plan. Where do I begin?

I need to put down the extra floor tiles in the furnace room to replace the ones that got damaged when I was working on the water leak. The extra firewood from that big load I bought last year needs to be moved down behind the house since it will be time to start using the basement fireplace again soon. I need to go buy a good wheelbarrow to move the wood (I will put this near the top of my list since I love excuses to go to the home improvement store). There is laundry that needs done (bottom of my list even though Sally may yell at me for not getting to it … she is gone for the day).

When Sally is gone it is important that I do a couple of things that will catch her eye when she comes home and makes her inspection. I know that she checks dishes and vacuuming and laundry. If I have made no progress in those areas, I am likely to be in her doghouse. I could spend a couple of hours at the store picking out the perfect wheelbarrow or the right set of socket wrenches for a project and yet she fails to see the value of my efforts, but throw some jeans in a drawer and then fold the top pair so that it looks really neat and she will think I am the best husband in all the land. I also know that Elizabeth wants to go to the mall with a friend later, so I will tell her to wash the dishes first and then she can go. I will hope that the subject never comes up and Sally will assume that I did those too! Anyhow, back to my list …

The computer chair sits on a painted cement floor in the basement. It has rubbed the paint off under it. I need to repaint that area and then go buy a mat to go under the chair (I could do that while I am out for the wheelbarrow … boy, I am smart!). I could even get something for lunch while I am out doing all of that shopping. I have been feeling kinda hungry and if I eat at home, I will just have more dishes to worry about. Let's see. I need to replace two ceiling tiles. I need to fix the basketball goal. It has been abused by the kids. The ping pong table needs reassembled. I meant to do it after that project six months ago. I need to tune my drums and take the heads off to put some muffling material inside. The refrigerator needs cleaned out (put that below washing clothes). I need to fix the old vacuum cleaner that we use downstairs. The yard needs mowed. The Jeep needs cleaned out. The upstairs sofa needs some structural work. The garage still has some junk that needs sorting to see what we will keep and what we will sell to some unsuspecting sucker at our next yard sale. I need to work on the spare computer. It has a virus. I need to reorganize the cable TV wires … Boy, this list is getting long. Just making the list is making me a bit tired. And it is Sunday, the day of rest, after all … and it is the end of September … and the Steelers are playing on TV in about an hour ... and I would like to eat pizza while I watch the game ...

Today, I made my list of things that needed done and I did some other stuff ... that's my story and I hope Sally buys it.

College Bound

I always thought that going to college would be a wonderful experience. Meeting new friends and opening the mind to new ideas and experiences sounded like a great thing. I saw college as an opportunity to spread your wings and grow into your potential. College was something to always work toward, a goal to achieve. Four years of intensive learning and growing always seemed like the best way to enter adulthood with a head of steam.

The trouble is that I never realized that college would sneak up on me so fast and that I would feel that it all came too quickly. Yes, Shelly, my daughter, moved away to college about six weeks ago and I miss her. I never took the time to realize that her going to college would mean her leaving me. After eighteen years she is gone and it will never be the same. Sure, she may be home in the summers for a while, but in the end it will be different. I am so very proud of her. She has become such a wonderful young woman. I will mourn the passing of her childhood, yet rejoice in the promise of her future.

UPDATE: It is now two years later and I have just delivered Elizabeth to Kent St. in Northern Ohio. Will is now running around the house incessantly singing Ding Dong the Witch is Dead! Me? I am sad again. Another kid has left the nest. This growing up bit is no fun for me! I am running out of people to play with!

ANOTHER UPDATE: Well, another two years have passed and this time Will has left me too. I took him up the interstate to the university of his choice and dumped him out. This doesn't get any easier! All that is left now is their spare stuff they didn't want and their pets. I think maybe I need to go to college too. FuzzButt can take care of things at home while I am gone.

Okay, now backward in time we go to tell secrets about these people who have abandoned their dear old dad. The kids are known to have said that you have to be careful what you do around dad or it may end up in a book! (Evil laugh)

Falling into Fall

Today is the first day it has felt chilly in many months. It is kinda breezy and the temp is in the 50's. I absolutely love this kind of weather. I always have more energy and just a better attitude when the weather is crisp like this. It summons up visions of piling up colorful leaves and jumping in them. The kids down the road had some big trees and lots of leaves. We would make huge piles and take a run at them from way up the hill around the house. We would take turns bounding down the hill at lightning speed and flying into a pile higher than our heads. One particular year I remember that their parents must have gotten a new appliance of some sort. There was a big box out by their garage. I had the one girl go up around the house and wait while I made her a special big leaf pile to jump in … NO PEEKING! I told her. I then dragged the huge box over and covered it in the leaves. Next, here she came flying down the hill! As she reached terminal velocity at the edge of the leaf mountain, she threw herself up into the air! It turned out to be a perfect jump, catapulting her right into the opened end of the hidden box buried in the leaves.

This time of year gets me to thinking about pumpkin pie and Halloween. A cool, crisp night. You get to wear funny costumes and the neighbors, even the grumpy ones, are all giving out candy! Well, there always is that one weirdo neighbor who gives out toothbrushes or little handmade pumpkins she made at ceramics class or sugar free fruit rollups. Always remember their house so you can go back and toilet paper their trees at a later date. WE WANT SUGAR!

I also get a strong urge about this time to go for a walk in the woods and spend the day. Many people do not fully comprehend what I mean by a walk in the woods. Today, most people go to parks with cleared hiking trails made through them. These are cool, but what I prefer is to get out into a woods on a farm where no human has ventured in months or even years. These are the places you discover all sorts of interesting things. Give me a sunny afternoon with a breeze and the temp around 70 and I will find a good fallen tree upon which to take a nap. Before and after napping, I find a sort of peace and serenity in this setting that I find nowhere else in the world. I will see the occasional critter going about its daily business of looking for food. Deer, squirrel, chipmunks and rabbits are a common sight. I even remember one time watching a fox playfully making his way along, completely unaware of my presence. I also like to just lay back and look upward through the trees and think about nothing , just taking in my surroundings. I cannot really explain why, but I always seem to return from one of these outings feeling less stressed and more at peace with the world. So if you are looking for me later today and I am nowhere to be found, just know that I am probably renewing my spirit out there somewhere in the middle of nowhere.

Evelyn's Basketballs

Evelyn is our deaf-blind daughter. She is a special kid with special needs. Her greatest love in the world is basketballs. Due to her autistic tendencies, we do not fully understand why she loves basketballs so much. She just does. And she doesn't like the cheap ones either! She can pick out the most expensive ball in a heartbeat and it has nothing to do with the price tag. She judges each one by touch and smell. I think she enjoys the aroma of a fine leather ball.

Evelyn is not totally blind. She does have some peripheral vision and she is able to use this limited sight to do some amazing things. Just get her within a mile of the sporting goods store at the mall and she will sneak off and navigate her way to those basketballs. At least it makes her easy to find when we lose her. And when we do catch up, there she will stand in awe of the ball wall. Soon she will begin examining each of them carefully before making her final selection of the perfect ball which she intends for us to purchase for her. Of course she does not always get to take it home, I mean, how many fifty dollar balls does one girl need?

She always seems to get a new ball for Christmas. It is funny to watch her surveying all of the wrapped gifts looking for one the right size and shape to contain the latest addition to her collection. If someone else has a gift under the tree which meets those specifications, you'd better watch out because Evelyn will open it the first chance she gets when she thinks nobody is watching.

From where I currently sit, I can see some of Evelyn's basketballs ... eleven of them to be exact. Out of all the balls, she has one all time favorite. It actually belonged to her older brother, Jarrod. It has his name written on it in fading permanent marker. Evelyn cherishes that ball. When it is misplaced she is highly stressed until we can find it. Sometimes retrieval is not so easy. She has been known to leave it at grandma's house or in a friend's car etc. ... On these occasions getting her ball back has been a top priority for days at a time. Once she has it back in her possession, she holds it close to her nose inspecting it inch by inch and taking in that aroma of old leather as if it were the most satisfying scent in the world. And in her world, maybe it is.

Being Unique

Each of us has a unique life experience. As much as we share, as much as we have in common, the subtle differences help to mould us into the individuals that we are. There are a million little things that we come to expect as normal in our day to day existence. We often take these things for granted. For instance, as I write on this computer, our cat, FuzzButt, always comes and sits on top of the monitor. Why is he there? He is waiting and watching to see if I am going to print anything. No, I am not kidding. He is absolutely fascinated with the printer. As soon as he hears it make a noise, he jumps down and gets his nose up close to where the paper comes out and peers inside with great anticipation. He gets so excited as the papers come flying out. I don't really understand why, but he just loves the whole experience.

Another bit of uniqueness around here is due to the fact that Evelyn, our deaf-blind daughter, loves to swing … not just a little bit … she swings for hours some days. The sensation for her is not just a want but a need. It is so important that I installed an indoor swing in the doorway leading from the upstairs living room to the hallway. She is often found happily swinging away at just about any time, day or night. Over time I have discovered that every member of our family gets on that swing at some point during the day. Even visitors seem to get in on the act. It has simply become a part of our normal. Another normal occurrence due to the swing is the "timed bathroom dash." There are two bathrooms and a laundry room down that hallway, and if Evelyn is swinging, she hates to be constantly disturbed by people coming through. So, to not interfere, we have all learned how to time our dash down the hall at the appropriate point in her swinging. You'd better not slack once you make your move either, or you will be bowled over by a foot in the butt.

The nightly challenge of what to cook for dinner is another unique experience at our house. With seven kids and two parents, the opinions are always varied yet the same. Elizabeth wants spaghetti, Shelly loves pizza, Lee wants steak, Will wants General Tso's Chicken, Jarrod wants tacos, Joannie wants whatever Will wants … or sausage gravy and biscuits, Evelyn wants hamburgers and Sally wants broccoli (yep, she's weird). As for me, I am sure you would agree that salmon patties make the best dinner of all time. What is constant is that no matter how many times I ask, the answers remain almost always the same. It is these things and a million more like them that make my world a unique place just as yours is unique to you.

Paige

Along with all of the children I have in my home, I also have a daughter that I have adopted as my own. Her name is Paige . She is at our house often and acts just like any of my other kids. She hugs me when she comes and hugs me when she leaves. She buys me gifts on special days and treats me like a dad. She just belongs right here with the rest of us in this crazy family we have. She is a big sister to all of the other kids here. She is present for most holidays and has even been known to just come over and help cook dinner. She is just a kid in her early twenties who is struggling to find her way in the world without a lot of support. All I know is that I am happy that my family and I can be her family too and I am truly blessed to have even one more daughter to love and cherish. I do indeed lead a charmed life.

Paige also has a dog. She calls him Kokiri. I think the name is from some online game or something. He is a cool dog. An Australian Cattle Herder. He is probably around sixty pounds or so. He is sort of an off white with brownish blonde patches and speckles. As a herding breed, he is highly intelligent. He knows many tricks. Shake, high five, lay down, sit, sit up, bite the mailman when he brings bills. He also herds everything! People, dogs, he tried herding the cats but that didn't work out too well for him. He is a good dog for Paige in the fact he is very friendly and loving, yet if someone ever tried to harm her, he would be a handful. What do I mean? Well, one time while we were babysitting him, I noticed that he could chew right through anything. At the pet store I found the guaranteed indestructible dog toy! I thought, boy I will show him! I think it took Kokiri 30 minutes to chew that thing to bits. An destructible dog Frisbee? One bite and it was punctured. That dog has some chops on him! Good thing he likes me!

Single Parenting

Today is a good example of life in my house of seven kids, four cats and three dogs. It is a Wednesday in early October. Sounds benign enough! But wait! This is MY world. Nothing is ever simple. Where do I start? Will (for the 3rd day) and Joannie (for the second day) are both home sick. They had the flu or something darned near like it. Fevers, coughing, sore throats, throwing up, etc. ... were all a part of their shared experience. They are on the mend now, but that just makes them more demanding of my services as maid, chief cook and bottle washer. I am waiting and watching for the mailman, UPS man, or FedEx man to bring me three important packages I have been waiting on. Progress is being held up here! It may soon cause an interruption in the space/time continuum. This is big stuff here! Well, at least it is to me! Maybe I am just a little stressed.

You see, my wife, Sally, is in Gettysburg this morning and on her way to Washington D.C. later today. She is on a business trip of sorts. She is a Sign Language Interpreter who is traveling with a deaf kid on an eighth grade field trip. She will be gone for five days. May the Lord take pity on my soul! Who cares about her troubles on a bus full of 13-year-olds! I am being torn to shreds by the demands of all of these rugrats right here at home! There are meals and laundry and dispute settlements and laundry and vacuuming and laundry and … well, you get my point. How could she do this to me! I am up to my ears in dirty dishes … and laundry. I need to mow the yard … and do laundry. Yet when she calls, I will have to act as if everything is running like a well-oiled machine. "No, no problems, all going great honey! Shut up Elizabeth! She doesn't need to know the firemen are here! Again! What's that honey? Oh nothing, just the kids playing video games. Me? Oh, not much, just watching TV and doing a little laundry. Hardly noticed you were gone." Whew! That was close!

By the way, if you are reading this would you please be on the lookout for Will? I gave him too much cough medicine and he was acting kind of loopy and now I cannot find him. He was saying something about all the pretty colors and then I got distracted and I am afraid he may have wandered off again. Sally is going to kill me if I lose one of these kids while she is gone!

What About Me?

Sally is complaining. She has been gone on the field trip with the eighth graders to Washington D.C. for two full days now and she is complaining that their schedule is insane. They left Indiana on Tuesday night, drove all night to Gettysburg, Pennsylvania (about a 12 hour trip by my calculation ... or 29, 872 miles according to Sally). Upon arrival they immediately toured the battlefields and then got back on the bus for Washington. They arrived in Washington and went to the National Cathedral and then on an evening tour lasting until about 11 P.M. By the time they got the kids to bed, it was midnight. This morning they rose at 6:30 and headed out to see the Capitol, Washington Monument, Jefferson Memorial, FDR Memorial, Ford Theater, Arlington, Smithsonian Air and Space Museum, Iwo Jima Memorial and a few other odds and ends. It is now 7PM and Sally texted me that she is tired. Awww! Poor baby!

Well let me tell you something! I am the one who had to sleep with Evelyn and Joannie all night because they came and crawled in my bed when I was not looking! Evelyn keeps a knee firmly planted in my back and Joannie sleeps sideways in the bed!

They are both cover hogs and Evelyn snores like her mother! I got so little rest last night that I had to take a two hour nap after I shipped them off to school this morning! I had to let the dogs outside three times today even though it was raining and they did not want to go! I even had to put frozen pizzas in the oven to feed all the rugrats when they got home from school today! Where's my pity? Who is feeling sorry for me?

The truth is that I am feeling sorry for me.

Golden Years

I have been noticing of late a lot of women who have hair that does not match their age. I do not know if hair technology has improved that much or if I am just paying attention more now. As we age, our hair tends to get more brittle and dull and just looks less vibrant. This is true of men and women. But now it is like hair is an avenue of hanging on to lost youth. This whole rant was brought on by an encounter I had today. I approached a woman who had her head down writing something at a service counter. My first impression of her from what I could see would have made her out to be maybe thirty years old. She had vibrant blonde shoulder length hair and was wearing clothing typical of a thirty year old. Yet when she raised her head to acknowledge me, I was confronted with a woman every bit of seventy-five and maybe even eighty! So either she was workin' very hard to retain part of her youth through hair and clothes or else she had lived one hell of a hard life.

Most of us wish we could be young forever for one reason or another. For me, it would be to have the energy I had at age 20. I am not as concerned about my ear hair and wrinkles. I just want to feel younger. It is different for everyone I guess. There are even some who prefer getting older. They say they enjoy the wisdom that comes with age. My favorite line about aging was often quoted by my father when in his seventies and eighties who said that he could not figure out what was so golden about those years.

Feeding the Tribe

In our home dinner is a massive undertaking. With anywhere from seven to ten hungry mouths to feed on a given night, you often feel like a short order cook in a busy cafe. We are like many families making a mix of traditional homemade dinners and convenient items from a box or the freezer. Most families can buy one box of some easy to throw together noodle mix and have plenty ... maybe even leftovers, but we have to make four to five boxes just to have enough to go around. Want homemade mashed potatoes? You'd better get busy! I would estimate that we peel about seven pounds of them for an average dinner ... and that is just one side dish! Want to roast a chicken? Better make room in the oven for three of them. Cookies? Our kids do not know what a cold homemade cookie tastes like. They eat them faster than we can make them. Last December I decided to give them a treat and make sausage cheese balls. I could not believe that they were all standing around staring at the oven waiting on the next batch to pop out. I would set out a heaping tray full of them only to see them disappear in under a minute.

The greatest thing to any member in this family when it comes to food is to find something that hardly anybody likes. It is the only way to be certain that you can come back for a second helping. Will and Sally love beets (I know, there must be something really wrong with them!). Shelly and me, we like rice pudding (we obviously have the more sophisticated tastes). Lee is the only real steak eater in the house. They all have their quirks. One kid puts barbeque sauce on everything, another uses ranch dressing all the time and another loves the hot sauce. There are even a few demented souls living here who put peanut butter on their pancakes and make grilled peanut butter and jelly sandwiches. SICK! I tell you they are SICK!

My Special Day

I have a birthday coming up later this week. I will be forty-seven years old, or as I prefer to view it, I will be celebrating the thirty-first anniversary of my sixteenth birthday. Elvis once said something to the effect that there were no such things as grown men, just little boys in big bodies. I agree. Even at my age, I still feel like a kid inside. I may have developed an ache or a pain or two, but I still want to go outside and play on a nice day and I usually do. I just look funny doing it. I don't run nearly as fast and it hurts more when I fall, but I am still right out there. I guess I get that from my dad. I remember him running through the woods with his cane in hand chasing my kids when he was eighty-five years old. He was laughing and smiling the whole way.

Getting older, to me, is not all bad. I do gain a lot from all of the experience I now have behind me. Another thing is that I am more comfortable with who I am. I can go to the store wearing old faded sweat pants and mismatched socks and not really care what anybody thinks about my attire … well take that back … Sally will order me to change before she leaves the house with me … silly, superficial girl. She is only forty-four. The wisdom wagon has not visited her door yet. Another couple of years and she will be heading out with messy hair and holes in her clothes just like me. I try to tell her all the time to just do as I say, but she is kinda stubborn. She has a birthday in December. I like reminding her that she will be halfway to ninety.

Anyhow, the birthdays just keep piling on and I just keep getting prettier. I call it Handsomer's Disease and I tell everyone that its getting worse every year. I am just one of the lucky ones I guess. I bet Sally is just jealous. Yep! I bet that is it! She is always shaving her legs and coloring her hair and slathering on creams and tweezing her eyebrows and me … I don't do any of those things and STILL look this good! She is certainly one lucky girl to have me!

My birthday has always been a celebration. Millions of people get all dressed up for the occasion! Kids say my birthday is one of their favorite days of the year. Sally just says that the fact that I was born on Halloween explains a lot. I am not sure what she means by that. Maybe it is because I am sweet like candy. Yep! I am certain that is it!

Enjoy Today

Here it is the evening of the 22nd of December. Christmas is just around the corner. Many people I ran into today were quite nervous or frazzled … some more than others. There were some cranky people out there too. I think the whole thing has just gotten the best of them. Time is running out and they realize they still have a lot to do to create that "perfect" holiday. I believe that therein lies the problem. We all get so hung up on trying to make things perfect that we often fail to stop and enjoy the moment.

This is not just true at Christmastime, but throughout the years of our lives. We often rush to get to a certain place either physically or emotionally' only to find that once we get there, we are already rushing toward the next thing. Where is the part where we take in the moment and enjoy it for what it is? Sometimes rushing things causes great harm as well. I am guilty of that one. You get in such a hurry that you actually damage the good things you already have. You can hurt people's feelings and damage friendships. I am willing to admit that I am sometimes a lunkhead, but sometimes it is already too late and the damage has been done.

So, I want you to slow down and enjoy today. It doesn't matter if it is Halloween or Christmas or Ramadan or just January 8th or March 9th. Celebrate today! Enjoy today! Tomorrow will be here soon enough!

Reflections

It is 8pm on December the 24th, Christmas Eve. I find this a great time for reflection on the things that really matter in life. This is one of the only times anymore when the commerce of the world slows to nearly a halt and we actually spend time celebrating with family and friends. That is a very good thing.

Of course the story behind this holiday has been retold many times over the centuries. We all know of the manger, and the wise men, and the birth that forever changed history, and the bright, shining star. That star was a real star and it generated its light from within. You also have the power from within to shine. You have the ability to leave a lasting impact on the world. We are blessed with that potential. It is up to each of us to realize it. You cannot allow the status quo mindset of the world to keep you from doing what you know in your heart is your calling. You have things you are passionate about, things you want to change in the world. It may be up to you to take charge in making those things better. If you are genuine and you lead, many will follow and help you along the way. You will face difficult times and you may not always see the light at the end of the tunnel. But, if you follow your heart and do what your inner light tells you is right, you will succeed in the end. It may not be the same success you envisioned when you started, but you will find your way to where you belong. Do not listen to those who say you can't. They are often wrong. Stay focused on what your heart tells you. You will know when the message is good and just. The lives you can touch and the history you can change by being true to your passions are immeasurable.

Voice to Text

It is the evening on Christmas Day. The gifts have all been opened, and the food prepared and consumed. Now is the best time of the day. It is a time to relax with family and friends, or to just settle in for a quiet, comfortable evening. As for me, I intend to settle into bed with one of my new books I received as a Christmas gift. I will be snuggled deep within my five new pillows. That's right, I received five pillows as gifts. I have made mention on a couple of occasions that the kids are notorious for stealing my pillows. Therefore, feeling sorry for me, multiple people bought me new pillows for Christmas. I will be able to settle in for a winter's nap with two pillows under my head, one between my knees and one between my ankles, along with the big body pillow I received running the length of my bed. And just let one of those little heathens try to steal my pillow now. I will have many reserves for ammunition in the event a pillow fight breaks out.

My other Christmas gifts consist of a container of honey in the comb, two books which I will thoroughly enjoy, a bathroom scale (I guess they think I'm getting fat) and a voice recognition program for my computer. This program allows me to speak my stories and the computer does all the typing. It really works quite well as long as I remember to speak in clear succinct tones. If I forget this and start just blabbering along, it may print all sorts of things. As an example, I will reread this paragraph in just a typical speaking voice. When I am finished, I will not edit the final result. I will be curious to see what it says. Okay, here goes!

My other Christmas gifts consist of container of hot honey in the column to books which I will thoroughly enjoy a bathroom scale against them getting fat and voice recognition program for my computer this program allows me to speak my stones and the computer does all the typing it really works quite well as long as I remember speaking clear sing tones if I forget and just our blabbering along it met all sorts of things as an example I will read this paragraph is a typical speaking voice when finished I will edit the final result of the Keirsey love says okay here goes!

Wow! That was fun! I will have to try that again sometime. Anyhow, I hope your Christmas was as good as mine.

Inside My Mind

I have been struggling recently with determining my place in life. I seem to struggle with the difference between the things I need to do, the things I want to do and the things I'm inspired to do.

The things I need to do are often boring, dull and mundane tasks. These are things like fixing that squeaky board of the hallway, repainting the trim around the doors of the house, or replacing the ceiling tiles that have water damage in the basement. It seems I have a million of these kinds of things to do. There are all sorts of things that need fixing or cleaning all around the house, the cars, in the yard and even my body. My body? Why of course. I am talking about things like trimming that hair that grows my ears. It seems like that is always needing done. The older I get the more that I need it.

Things I want to do often take more time and money than I have to invest. Some of them are quite simple. For instance, I love to play racquetball. This is not an expensive pastime, but it takes time and I have to find someone else who wants to play with me. I would also like to go out and play music more in public. I would even enjoy going to a karaoke bar to sing on occasion. For those things, it is mostly a matter of time with the lack thereof which present the problem. I do have things I want to do which cost much money. I would love to spend a summer playing golf on the links courses of northern England and Scotland. I also want to just bum around living in a beach house for a month or two. Of course, life tends to get in the way of those types of things.

Things I am inspired to do are neither dull nor boring. They do, however, require a great dedication of my time and energy. The difficult part would be how to do this and still be able to care for the needs of those who depend on me. I often like to look at the world from beyond the perspective that mankind has created for me. We tend to get caught up in our own little worlds and forget that there are those who have immensely less than we do. I often wonder if I am too selfish to give up my life as it is now to pursue what I would call a greater good for the world at large. There are so many needs. There are impoverished children who have nothing. There are animals that are abandoned, tortured, and killed for no good reason. There is human suffering in many areas of the world that we cannot even fathom. Yet we sit here with our bellies full in our warm houses with all the creature comforts one could possibly imagine while those with nothing suffer. I am inspired by the dreams and accomplishments of others and I hope to soon sort out what is the best way for me to help as well.

Maybe it is because it is Christmas, well the day after Christmas, but the same season which often brings this sort of thoughts. Perhaps if the days were longer, I would have time to accomplish all of these things. I could fix the sink in the morning, play a little golf in the afternoon, stop by and make dinner for children in the evening. If only that were true. Instead, I will have to try to work out a compromise that I can live with.

My Wandering Mind

I enjoy talking to people. When you keep your mouth closed and listen, you can learn a lot. I had a friend tell me that the human mind comprehends speech at a much higher rate than we actually speak. The problem is, this allows our minds to wander, therefore missing the details of what is being said. I found that to be quite interesting.

I think this might explain a lot. I could use this to explain all sorts of problems when it comes to multitasking. The next time one of the kids tells me that they need lunch money for school and I forget to send it, I could blame it on the fact that I was just engrossed in thought about what a handsome young man or woman this child had become. Surely they will buy this reasoning. I wonder if this line of thought would work as well when I forget to pay the electric bill on time. "I am so sorry ma'am! I was so caught up in admiring the quality of your service that the thought of paying the bill simply slipped my mind! I know you can understand." Forget someone's birthday? "Oh Sarah! You are so active and youthful looking. It never even crossed my mind that you could be that old!" Get stopped for speeding ticket? "I'm sorry officer, I was just very anxious to get by the doughnut shop to pick up a little something to drop off at the police station. I didn't even realize I was speeding."

This whole wandering mind thing is something that seems to become a much larger problem the older I get. Combine that with the fact that I don't hear very well and I often get into trouble even when I don't intend to. I will sometimes go to the grocery store needing to pick up five things. The trouble is when they told me what they needed, I only heard three of them and two of the ones I heard, I heard wrong. So instead of paper towels, milk, Colby cheese, white rice, and potatoes, I will come home with cottage cheese, white rice (hey! I got that one right!) and tomatoes. When I get home, they look at me like I'm nuts. Of course, not being able to hear too well, I am spared all of the comments I am sure they are making behind my back. So I just go on my merry little way in my own little world, content in the fact that I went out and brought home the white rice.

Expect the Unexpected

Happy New Year! Wow, that makes me feel old. A new year is supposed to be a sort of checkpoint in our human civilization, a time to take stock in what is good and what is bad in our lives. A time to look forward with anticipation and, hopefully, with a plan of how to make things better. Many people will have resolutions to lose weight or quit smoking or go to church more. Many will simply look at it as a new beginning to reenergize their efforts to grow in their careers or their personal lives. There is nothing wrong with having these goals. Even if you fail to realize complete success, you may move toward something better.

As for me, I enter the new year with no real resolutions, only confusion. There are many fronts in my life where I have no idea which way to turn or what to do. I do not mind SOME uncertainty, but I enter the new year with ALOT of it. This is shaping up to be a year of massive change in both my public and private life. I am very curious what my life will look like as I enter 2011. Oh well, I guess I had better just buckle my seatbelt and enjoy the ride!

You see, there will be both good and bad in the coming year. That is true for most of us. That is just how life is. The important thing is to enjoy the journey as much as possible. I know that some of the bad stuff is tough to take, but you need to learn and grow from even those experiences. Also, do not be in a rush to get to the end result of the good times either. Take your time and enjoy the journey. The best parts are often found along the way and not at the final destination. If you look back on life, it is most often those unplanned, unexpected moments that mean the most. So, even though I expect much turmoil in the coming year, there will also be those surprises that I cannot even begin to imagine that will occur and for me that is the best part of living.

Wasting

Let me see if I can give you a small sampling of the things I have on my mental agenda as of late. I cannot give you a complete list as that would take up way too much time and energy. I want to make a set of wooden salad bowls in my woodshop (supposed to be a winter project, but winter is half over), go through those totes in the garage (ditto), go out and meet with some individuals regarding a business venture I am starting with a few friends, go to Pennsylvania and fix the bedroom ceiling at grandma's house, record Herb's song … My friend Herb gave me some lyrics he had written a few years ago and asked me to put music to it. I did that a month ago, but I need to record it and send it back to him. I need to finish that new Mitch Albom book I got for my birthday, fix the scoreboard in Lane's basketball goal, teach Elizabeth how to do a demo (she is playing guitar and writing songs and wants to see what happens with them), retune my drums and practice, find a band to play those same drums. I have not played much in public in recent years, but I want to do that again. You might say I have the itch. I need to call the mortgage company (that will take half a day in itself) and find new homeowner's insurance (my old one canceled me because I actually had a claim for damage from a hailstorm). Insurance companies don't seem to want customers who actually use the insurance when something bad happens. I need to do the customary 100,000 mile oil change on my old Jeep. It runs great, but I don't want to take any chances.

It's just one thing after another. Sure, I could complain about it. I could say that I am too busy. I could moan that life is unfair. But that would simply be wasting time. When you think about it, in the end, time is the only thing that we have that matters. I can print more money in the basement ... er ... I mean ... I could work more hours at a second job or something to make more money. I could move to some religious cult and get extra wives to do the chores. But there is nothing I can do to get more time. You are given one lifetime. Period. I recall reading famous last words in a book. There was a queen in England who said "All of my possessions for one more moment of time." I mentioned money. If you waste it, you can make more. Time is different. If you waste it, sorry, it is just gone. Do not waste one single moment.

Spooky

I was at the hardware store and there was a lady who came in looking for a headlight flashlight. She stated that she was looking for one with an infrared light in it. Personally I have never seen one like that. Next, she was looking for a thermometer which uses an infrared beam to measure the temperature wirelessly across the room. That seemed like an odd combination of items. It was then that she stated her reason for needing these items. She confessed that in two weeks she was going on a trip to an old abandoned hospital ghost hunting. She said the infrared light makes it easier to see the ghosts. She also stated the infrared to monitor measures the slight temperature changes caused by ghosts in the room. She was convinced that this hospital she was going to was "full of ghosts and spirits." Who am I to doubt her?

Freeloading Mutts

I should have known I was in for trouble! I should have seen it coming!

The other day Sally came in and said, "There were two dogs running loose up the street and they came out of the woods and started a fight with our dog when we were on a walk!"

I should have known better when she went on to say how beautiful they were and how they must surely belong to somebody. I should have realized that somebody would end up being me!

Sally has given me daily reports on her sightings of these two stray mutts and has been spending a lot of energy worrying about their potential fates. Well, this morning she called me at work to let me know that the dogs were encamped on our porch. I wonder, out of all the thousands of houses in my suburban neighborhood, how did they choose mine? I think I need to check the refrigerator for those leftover pork chops from the other night. Something sure seems funny to me! As the day went on I received reports about how sweet these two freeloaders were and how hungry they had been.

"They ate three bowls of food!" Sally said proudly.

I tried to explain to her that if you feed them they won't leave. I guess I was just in denial. By the time I got home, these two hoodlums had their own food and water bowls and new collars! Sally even had an old blanket in the dryer preparing it for the evening! They now have names, although not the ones I chose for them. Sally said I was being mean and cruel! She even suggested that perhaps the dogs should sleep in her room and that I should be the one sleeping outside on the blanket!

Losing to the Dogs

Well, the last time I wrote, Sally had been feeding two strays. Now, ten days later, these two "strays" live in my garage and the one even seems to end up in the house some of the time. Sally has named them, bought them collars and leashes and feeds them dinner leftovers, sometimes even before I get home to have my turn to eat, leaving me with the leftover leftovers that not even these freeloading dogs will consume. She claims she is actively seeking a new home for them, but I have not seen any prospective owners lining up outside my door. I have even come home to find Sally curled up napping with the one dog. She doesn't even do that with me anymore. And to have those two mutts take over my garage? I had turned that into my mancave! It was my escape from Sally's chores. I would sneak out there and hide for an hour or two at a time claiming to be working on some important project. Now I go out there and just get slobbered on and growled at. I was saving that old living room chair out there for my mancave TV room, now it is just disgustingly covered in dog hair.

I wish that Sally could see the truth. It is me she should be scratching behind the ears and I would love to have my tummy rubbed and why can't she bring me a treat from the store or give me a warm bath? Heck, I won't even bark in the middle of the night to wake her when I need to go to the bathroom.

Troubles are a Comin'

Here it is the 3rd of February. This is just about as deep into the dark, cold winter as you can get. By this time most of us are pretty much ready for the warmth of spring, ready to get outside and get busy. But, yesterday that goofy groundhog said that we would have six more weeks of this misery.

As for me, I am feeling like a sloth. I can't ride my bike or play Frisbee or bocce ball with the kids or cook on the grill … well, I guess I could, but you see, I enjoy laying on the hammock while the stuff cooks and that just does not sound inviting, considering the fact that it is like twenty degrees outside today.

Once spring arrives I will be able to get out in the fresh air. Of course Sally will have some ideas of how I should spend my time as well. She seems to think that I should enjoy mulching and planting and mowing and trimming and pruning and weeding and, well, the list seems endless. She even has this silly idea that I should climb the ladder and wash the outside of our windows. I tried to explain to her that God made rain to do that for us. She said that rain falls straight down and does not do the job properly.

"Well, not when it is windy!" was my brilliant response.

Sally then just shook her head and stormed off to the other room to clean something. You know, I think that maybe six more weeks of winter is not such a bad thing after all.

Post Super Bowl Blues

Well, here it is! The Super Bowl is over. The Saints are the champs and I am feeling empty. It is not because of who won or lost that I am feeling down, but just the mere fact that it is over. It is the same feeling I get on December 26th or November 1st. The holiday, the climax has been reached and now its back to square one again.

I enjoy watching NFL football. I have been a Steelers fan since 1972 when I became an official member of Franco's Italian Army. That was a fan club of sorts for Franco Harris, the Steelers' star running back at the time. I can sit down and watch a game no matter who the two teams are. I enjoy the drama and the strategy involved in playing the game. It is also a good excuse to eat things that are bad for me. "I know my cholesterol is up, but the game is on! Give me another bratwurst!" Football has turned out to be a good excuse for a lot of things. "I will have to rake those leaves tomorrow, the game is coming on." or "Can you cook dinner tonight? I would hate to miss kickoff and jinx the team."

There are many fans who have rituals they feel compelled to follow in order to help the team win. They will wear the same shirt or sit in the same chair or eat the same food game after game so as not to mess with their team's mojo. They somehow would feel responsible for the misfortunes if their team lost due to something they did not do. I can see it now!

"Tom Brady, how do you explain your team's heartbreaking loss today?"

"Well Curt, it all happened because Harry Wilson's wife forgot to buy him the lucky cheese dip at the store. That is the second time in three years! When will he wise up and divorce her so that we can win another Super Bowl?"

Since football has expanded, I have been able to avoid most of my chores for six months out of the year. All it takes is a little planning. With games on 3 or 4 days a week there are many opportunities for being lazy. But now here I am facing the long off season. I am worried. Sally has been making a list and checking it twice! A chore list that is! Good thing for me that the hockey playoffs will be starting soon!

No Respect

We, like many Americans east of the Mississippi River, have had more than our fair share of snow recently. It was pretty to watch it fall. It created a beautiful scene out our large picture windows overlooking the back yard and woods. It was nice to sit by the fireplace and enjoy a Winter's nap and sip on some hot cocoa. Sally and I even took a nice walk or two in the falling snow. It was fabulous. Sally told me that she loved the snow and loved being out in it.

For this reason I was quite surprised to find Sally waiting on me the next morning when I arose from my slumber. There she stood with snow shovel in hand. I told her that I would hate to see her go out and ruin all of that pristine beauty of the freshly fallen snow.

"I'm not!", she said.

Sally then went on to make it abundantly clear that it was my job as protector of the family to go out and shovel the driveway and sidewalk to make it safe for the rest of the family to get to the car so they could go to the mall. I asked who was gonna go out and make it safe for me? She just gave me that dirty look she gives when she thinks I have said something stupid. I then tried to explain the virtues of patience to her and that it would all melt away on its own in a week or so if we just left it alone! Again, I got the look.

Seeing that there was no winning this argument, I decided to change my tactics. Surely I could get something out of this deal. I told Sally that simply because I loved her sooooo much I would go out and make the driveway a pristine, snow-free cement landscape. The only thing I asked was that when I came back inside could she rub my tired feet.

"What do I look like? Your servant?" she said, seemingly insulted. "Besides, you will have plenty of time to rub your own feet before you cook dinner."

Sally fears that her dog may be pregnant. We decided we need to know for sure. So, right now Sally is chasing the dog around the yard carrying a Clear Blue Easy stick.

My Broken Heart

Today is Valentine's Day. Do you want to know what Sally gave me? Some candy, some cologne, and a broken heart. I know, I know, but it is the terrible truth that Sally broke my heart on Valentine's Day. She literally broke it into about eighteen pieces. She said it still tasted ok though.

Yes, the big day came. Her moment of truth. She went to flip my heart-shaped buckwheat pancake and she broke it in half! Then she went to flip it again and she broke it some more! I think she enjoyed it, because she kept flipping and breaking and flipping and breaking! By the time it hit the plate, all I had left was a heart-shaped buckwheat pancake puzzle! It was a reminder of what Humpty Dumpty must have looked like when the kings men found him. She was right about it still tasting good, but I will forever stick to the story that Sally broke my heart on Valentine's Day.

Dog Delivery

I had mentioned recently that Sally was caring for two stray dogs. I had become concerned that there might not be enough food to go around and that I was at the bottom of Sally's list when it came to dinner. Well, my fears are now all gone!

Early last week, Sally announced that she had found a new home for the male dog ... again ... and that the man would be by to pick him up. I, of course, assumed that she was just telling me another story to keep me off her back about it. As it turned out, I was pleasantly surprised when the man and his wife showed up one morning and hauled that freeloading mutt away. They seemed like great people and they were the type who will spoil him rotten. It almost made me wish that I was the one who was going.

The excitement began two days later when the two dogs original owner responded to an ad on Craig's list. They had been searching for their lost dogs! Except, oops! Sally had now had them spayed and neutered and found one a new home! Fortunately the old owner was very understanding and was happy just to take the female dog back.

The day we went to meet the old owner to make the exchange, the lady brought along her other dog. it looked to be a mix between a pit bull and a Clydesdale except meaner looking. Sally got out of the car to make the exchange. I thought better of the idea and stayed put in my seat with the window rolled up. The lady seemed unconcerned that the horse was staring at Sally with drool running down its lips and a hungered look on its face. She remained unconcerned when the doghorse jumped up on Sally to get a closer sniff and then began to growl. Sally had the same look on her face as the old gazelle in those Wild Kingdom shows who could no longer run fast enough to escape the lion. The lady was interested in chatting a bit. Sally was only interested in escaping with her arms and legs intact. Me? Oh I was just enjoying the show. I was, however, ready to drive Sally to the hospital at a moment's notice. I am a good husband like that.

Never Settle

I am one tired old man tonight. I have been going steady since about 630 this morning and it is now nearly 10pm. The days are never long enough, not to mention that there are far too few of them in one lifetime. I will never have time to even finish the ever-growing chore list that Sally has for me before my time is up in another forty or fifty years let alone do all the fun stuff I want to do.

Today was a day full of work for me, but it was "fun" work. That makes it a little better. I just seem to have a very busy life these days. I am lucky. I am healthy and hopeful and generally happy. That is much more than many can say. I lead a charmed, blessed life. Sure, I have troubles of one sort or another just like anybody else, but the good far outweighs the bad. I have no good reason to complain much. Of course I will always have to complain a little to Sally or she will get a big head, but that is just to keep her straight. But, overall my only regret is that life's glorious adventure is too brief. I feel very strongly that one should never pass up the opportunity to follow one's dreams and to reach for the things that you know in your heart are your passions. Never settle.

Women

Is it just me or is it true that the older a woman gets, the more perfume she wears? Well, let me take that back. Young girls often wear heavy doses of the stuff and then learn over time to tame it down. Many women wear what I would call a subtle hint of fragrance, but then what happens? I was in a store the other day and this lady of advanced years passed me and I was still smelling her when she was eight aisles downwind. I should have caught up with her and thanked her for cleaning out my sinuses. I could not help but wonder how she stood to ride in the car with herself. Were her senses that diminished?

Another thing that bothers me is when an old lady is in the grocery store and all of the sudden has a thought. It always happens when people are behind her trying to get through. As soon as that thought hits her she just stops dead in her tracks and ponders it a while. Apparently old women are incapable of walking and pondering at the same time. While this pondering is occurring, they also seem oblivious to others around them. All you really can do is just wait them out. Usually, after about ten seconds, they will lower their chin again and go on their merry way as if nothing ever happened.

I am just glad that old men have no such annoying habits.

Impatient

I am blessed with being an impatient personality. What I mean by that is that I see no sense in waiting until tomorrow to do what you can easily go ahead and do today, like making a decision. You can postpone and make excuses all you want, but eventually you gotta bite the bullet and decide! Do not get me wrong! It is a good thing to make informed decisions and to understand your options, but at some point additional analysis is simply a waste of time.

I have seen in my life people who would drive all over town investigating an item and spending $10 in gas for fear that if they checked one more store it just might be fifty cents cheaper. I also know of people who analyzed something for so long that the opportunity presented to them ended up passing them by. They would rationalize it by saying, "Well, I guess it wasn't meant to be." I think they simply missed an opportunity by being too afraid to commit.

There! I feel much better now!

Tater Salad Taxes

Mamaw, my mother-in-law, is at the top of my list today! No, not THAT list! She is at the top of my GOOD list! How did she get there? Well, she is always near the top of my good list. You see, she is the one who keeps telling Sally what a catch I am and how lucky she is to have such a great guy for a husband. Sally is not always so sure that she agrees, but who is she to go against her own mother? Sally says that Mamaw does not see the dirty clothes I leave on the floor or the shaved whiskers left in the sink or the mud I track in on my boots. I tell Sally that Mamaw simply sees past that to the person I am inside. Sally thinks Mamaw is looking way too deep.

Anyhow, back to my story. Mamaw had me to do her taxes last year. After a bit of creative ingenuity, I was able to parlay her 47 dependents ... after all we all depend on Mamaw for something don't we? Anyhow, those 47 dependents translated into a nice, big refund check. What did that mean for me? Tater Salad! What better way to show a Mamaw's love than to pay me with a big 'ol bowl of Tater Salad. Mamaw makes the best Tater Salad in the civilized world. So, why does that make me happy today, a year later? Well, Mamaw sent her tax papers home with Sally yesterday ... along with a down payment of ... you guessed it ... Tater Salad!

Discovering Potential

I have a friend who is taking a plunge soon. They are getting ready to go to a disadvantaged country to do some missionary work. She is facing fear of the unknown right now. But, I am willing to bet that once she goes, she will be so happy that she did. It is often difficult to put yourself out there to try new things, even when you know it is the right thing to do. But, to me at least, embracing those challenges in life is what living is all about. So get out there and take a few chances. You never know what opportunities may come your way.

In her case she is twenty-one and full of wide eyed ambition. She isn't exactly sure what she is going to do with all of that, but I keep telling her that she has the ability at this point in life to dream great big and then not listen to anyone who tells her she can't. She is articulate and creative and very capable. Her first hurdle will be her own self-confidence. If she doesn't lose sight of the big picture, she can do great things in her lifetime. I hope she discovers that potential I see in her.

Stop, Look, Listen

I have decided I need to live more in the moment. Too many of us are in a rush to get to some future event. Yet, once we get there, we don't even hardly pause to enjoy it before we are looking ahead to the next coming event. This is true of even fairly mundane things. I know people who spend all week at work looking forward to the weekend and then once the weekend arrives, they spend most of that time cringing at the thought of having to return to work on Monday. We want to rush to the end of a day or to get to a certain holiday or event. The problem is that we fail to enjoy the journey and therefore miss out on the best parts of life. On a sunny day, do you take a few moments to just enjoy that simple pleasure of warmth? In the shower, do you pause and enjoy the wonderful massage the water is giving you? When your kid comes to you and tells you something about what happened at school today, do you stop and truly listen? Those are important things! I believe they may be the true key to enjoying a fruitful and fulfilling life.

As I have pondered this notion, I have come to realize that there are many other things that should be enjoyed more fully as well. I have discovered literally hundreds of things we take for granted each day. For instance, all of those dandelions in the yard are not truly a menace, but a flower to be cherished. I should no longer be in a rush to run out there and rid my yard of this natural gift of a beautiful flower garden. Also, who says those are weeds in my garden? Those are just different varieties of plants vying for their own little place in the world. I should lay in my hammock and admire their beauty for awhile. My wife, Sally … I should admire her for the beautiful creation that she is even when she starts yelling at me for not doing my yard work. I will know that she is merely yelling at me with love in her heart

Swinger

I am working on building a swing for our daughter Evelyn today. It is her birthday and the thing that she enjoys most in the whole wide world is swinging. She has an indoor swing and an outdoor swing but I decided it was time for a slightly larger outdoor swing. Sally thinks that I may have gone a bit overboard. She seems to think that because the apex of the swing frame is slightly taller than the roof of our house that there is a problem. I tried to explain to her that the taller the swing, the longer the ride. Sally seems to think that at the height I am currently building that one round trip out and back may take Evelyn approximately thirty minutes. I say just send a sandwich with her and she will be fine. Sally also has this way of projecting her doubts in my abilities. She says things like "Are you sure that is the right kind of lumber?" or " I remember the swing we used to have used 2x6s. Are those boards smaller? Are you sure those will not break?" I am building a swing set that would hold a 600 pound man and Sally is worried that Evelyn, who is all of 100 pounds, may be too much for it. Sally says I have to watch out for the septic tank fingers and to be sure to dig out the legs and put cement around them. I am beginning to think that she has no faith in my abilities. She sure is doing good at bossing me around. Maybe I should do a structural integrity test by stringing Sally up out there by her ankles and leave her there until morning.

    I swear I can't get anything done these days because I just have too much to do! I run 90 mph from dawn til midnight and never seem to get caught up! It is a good thing though. I am vibrant and active in so many things. Sally thinks I am not always active in the correct things. It seems her list of stuff I should be doing is quite different from my list. I have a lot of projects that I have started which do not include cleaning or repairing something and she seems to disagree with that. She does not seem to understand that I am a man of vision and ideas. I just do not know if I will ever get her trained properly.

Aging Gracefully

I am not so sure I like this whole aging thing. It is just seems to change your whole outlook on things. Being in my late forties, those who are older would say that I am still just a kid. Yet, when I have a shoe that is untied, I would beg to differ with them. It goes something like this …

Hmm … My shoe feels kinda loose. Let me lean over here and see if I can notice if anything is wrong. Ok, just a second. Let me get my glasses on. Yep it looks to be coming untied. Is it that bad or will it maybe hang in there until I get home? It's a long way down there and my back is kinda stiff today. I sure would not have put on this pair of jeans today had I known my shoe would come untied. How did they get so tight anyway? When I lean over they feel like a tourniquet around my waist. Now, what was I doing? Oh yes, my shoe. If I get down there my pants may cut off circulation and cause even more trouble. My arms must be getting shorter or my legs longer. What's the worst that could happen if I just leave it that way? All I know is that my next pair of shoes is gonna have Velcro.

Wait, did I just wish for Velcro shoes? Oh God, I am getting old!

As time goes by, I have come to realize that the best things in my life are the lasting friendships that I have with a mere handful of people. My life has seen many major changes. But, there are certain people who have always been there and probably always will be. There can even be a period of a few years where there is no communication. The good thing is that as soon as you reconnect, it is like you were never really apart. These few people are the ones who on a moment's notice would do just about anything for me, as I would for them. So, just take a moment today to reconnect with one of those people in your own life. I am certain you will be glad you did.

Understanding a Woman

I am very tired today. I have been running full steam for many days now with little sleep. This often happens when I am passionate about a project and have my creative juices flowing. Such is the case right now. When I get focused on something, I keep at it until I get it figured out. My wife, Sally, says the problem for me is that when I get focused on something, I tend to forget everything else … like my chores, for example.

Sally has been complaining that I haven't been doing my share of the dishes and housework and kid tending and stuff. I thought that was what I married her for … just don't tell her I said that. I am currently in the doghouse for something I already said that she took offense to. I am always saying the wrong things around her and my opinions often get me into trouble. This latest time, she told me I was immature. Heck I already knew I was a kid in a grown-up body, so why is she so mad about that all of the sudden? She also said that I didn't understand her. Heck, I already knew that too! I have not understood most of the things women do since about age 12. I asked her to explain to me what she was mad about and she said I would have to figure it out on my own. Figuring things out on my own and forming an opinion about them is what got me into this mess in the first place!

Geese

My mother is a feisty old woman. At 84-and-one-half years old, she recently completed a stint as a census worker, not really because she needed a job, but because she has been a census worker every time for the past fifty years or so. I get many things from her. We both are the type who believe we can do anything in this world if someone just shows us how. I also get that internal drive that refuses to take no for an answer or refuses to believe that something simply cannot be done. That one has sometimes gotten both of us into trouble. But the greatest gift that I received from my mother is the strong compulsion to be the caregiver to animals in need.

Growing up with her, I was always involved in treating some wounded animal or medicating some stray cat ... have you ever attempted to ram a full sized penicillin capsule down the throat of a wild cat? It is an interesting experience, to say the least. Another thing she always did was stop for the turtles in the road. We would either get out and simply move them to the other side or else throw them in the car and haul them to our house before releasing them. Most of these were land or box turtles, but I actually recall hauling a snapping turtle or two as well. When you are six, you feel about like the crocodile hunter guy who used to be on TV. I even remember one time as a teenager attempting to beat a semi truck to a turtle in the street. I was yelling at mom that a truck was coming and she was yelling back "Hurry up and get that turtle!" I even own a cat today who I rescued from the middle of an interstate. Where am I leading with this story?

Well, this morning I had to take my old Jeep to the car mechanic to have them check out a strange squeak it was making. The guy said it would take about an hour to get me taken care of, so I told him I would walk down the street for some food and then return. This place sits on a very busy divided four lane street plus turning lanes. There is even a curb-high divider in the middle of the street to limit where people can turn. So, I walk outside and immediately was thrust into action to help a guy who was in the middle of this busy street with cars whizzing by trying to help out two Canadian geese and their five babies who were stuck in by the curb. The babies were too small to jump over the curb, the parents were trying to get them moving, the cars were honking their horns and flying by. It was a mess! A disaster in the making. Anyhow, I go out into the street. I try to get cars to stop. The other guy is herding the geese toward the side of the road. The father goose then took offense to my intrusion on the whole situation and flew at me and started biting me on the back … well, he was really getting mostly shirt and he has no teeth, but he meant business all the same. Finally, we got the geese up into the grass and on their way toward an office park with lots of grassy areas. Disaster averted! … Well, not so fast … For unknown reasons (men my age tend to wander aimlessly at times), I went back into the car mechanic place and sat down to read a magazine. I guess I had forgotten I was hungry. I had been there about five minutes and

I looked up and out the window and there was the goose family again attempting to cross the same road! Again, cars whizzing by, horns blowing etc. … Only this time my human helper was long gone. I was on my own! I went flying out the door and dashed into the busy street once again to retrieve my adopted goose family. The father goose again was none too happy to see me and let me tell you , the feeling was mutual. Once again we tangled a time or two as I prodded his little family to get back into the grass.

This whole fiasco went on three or four more times. Every time I would start to walk away, they would head back toward the street. I eventually had to find a goose herding stick and coax them two blocks into the office park complex before they finally gave up and walked the other way. This whole episode took about forty-five minutes.

So see it is all my mom's fault! She made me stubborn and made me be that person who refuses to accept defeat and made me to care for the animals even at risk of my own life and limbs, but I will tell you that I do feel pretty darned good tonight knowing that that silly geese are not splattered in the street. Thanks mom!

Mechanics

I went to the mechanic yesterday. It is kinda like going to the dentist. It is often a painful experience. I cannot recall the last time I went to the mechanic and he said, "No big deal, Mr. Hewitt! It was just a loose bolt. You owe us $8.49 for the 5 minutes it took to fix the problem."

No, no, no! They always tell me that I will be in grave danger to drive my car another inch and that it is purely a miracle I made it to the shop without losing life or limb to this deathtrap I drive, but for $784 plus tax they can make it as good as new in about 90 minutes. They must perform miracles back there because when I read my bill I have 7 hours of labor charges all performed in 90 minutes. I am guessing that they must have had the whole staff stop what they were doing just to work on my car! Don't I feel special?

Yard Sale Mania

Tomorrow is yard sale day for me. I love going to yard sales. It is like a treasure hunt except you never know what sort of treasure you are even looking for until you spot it. I find all sorts of cool stuff out there. I am amazed at what people are willing to part with for a buck or two. Sally says I am a cross between the absent minded professor and Fred Sanford. She says I go out and buy all of this "junk" and then forget I even have it in the garage when I need it, therefore making an unnecessary trip to the store to spend money. I tell her that she is missing the point. I bring her and the kids stuff too. Did she not appreciate the Football bloopers movie I got for our son? Oops, that's right … she said we got him the same one for Christmas. Or how about the patio set with the broken chairs I intend to fix for her someday? I got the whole set for like five bucks! Sure it takes up space in the garage, but who puts their cars in there anyway? I bought that big box of old computer cords too and I am more than willing to share those! Then there is the padded folding chair. I am not really sure where to put it in the house but it is still a great chair. I find gadgets and gizmos that keep me entertained in my mancave (the garage) and I take great pleasure in that. I can spend hours out there just tinkering around on stuff. Instead, Sally wants me to fix the mower again. Where is the fun in that? As soon as I get it fixed, she will want me to go use it on the yard for two or three hours. I tell her it would be more ecofriendly to let the grass grow and then bail it and take it to some farmer to feed cows during the winter. I am just a caring guy like that. Besides, the lawnmower and weedeater just harm the ozone with their emissions. When I go in the garage I am actually recycling old things and not polluting anything. I think I should qualify for some of those green government tax credits for the time I spend out there. Ok, ok, I know I got off track there. Back to the yard sales.

I love them because you meet a lot of friendly people. You get to look for treasures and you get to spend the morning kind of oblivious to the stresses of the world. To me that is a great escape and I am looking forward to it. Maybe I will find a good deal on a goat too!. Sally will be so proud! The yard will be mowed regularly and the kids will have a new pet!

Scheduling

I don't sleep like I used to. When I was a teenager, I could put in a good 12 or 14 hours as if I were in a coma. Nothing would awaken me. Mom said I slept like a bump on a log ... whatever that means. Nowadays it seems that I sleep with one eye open all of the time. Any little disturbance and I am awake for an hour just laying there. On top of that, I just can't seem to get comfortable. My hand is in the wrong position or my pillow isn't conforming to the shape of my head just right or my knees are rubbing together or the cat has jumped on the bed and is now attacking my toes which are protruding from the covers. The bottom line is that I am tired! I long for that bump on a log feeling of my youth. I have heard people say that you just don't sleep as well when you get older. I think that maybe you have to just adjust your sleeping habits a bit.

You see, I have been pondering this matter a bit and I have come to realize that there are times that I sleep just fine! Put a movie on the TV and I am out like a light in 10 minutes or less. I can tell you how lots of movies begin, but the endings? ... well, that part is a little more fuzzy. Also on TV, the third quarter of a football game will do it to me. I fill up my belly at halftime and then my third quarter nap soon follows. I also tend to doze off during Sally's lectures about the virtues of doing my chores and of finishing the things I have started. She seems to get a little angry when I break into a loud snore in the middle of her preaching.

 I do find that a nap about 2 in the afternoon goes over well with me, but it makes me kinda sluggish the rest of the day. It just seems to remove the ambition I had for getting stuff done. I guess I could still find it in me to at least start a few more projects.

 There! I have a plan. Up at 8. Eat breakfast and read paper 'til 9 then plan my day. Snack at 10 then check email etc.. 'til 11. Begin a specially chosen job for the day in the mancave (garage). Lunch at 12. Nap 1-3. Ponder how best to continue with mancave project 3-4. Afternoon snack 4-430. Plan dinner 430-5. Run to grocery store 5-6. Cook dinner 6-630. Eat dinner 630- 7. Clean up mess made in mancave from starting project earlier in day 7-8. Watch a movie 8-815. Take a movie nap 815 - 10. Shower/shave 10-1030. Go to bed 1030. Seems like a full schedule to me.

Free Labor

I get to have ALOT of fun this morning! I get to do the most exciting thing! Yep, I get to help someone move! Don't you just love all of the packing and lugging and breaking and cleaning and … well it's just more fun than a sack of rocks, yes it is!

There is one part of this experience I will enjoy. I get to drive the big truck. Nobody messes with you when you are driving the big truck. They take a wide berth around you and you ALWAYS have the right of way. I remember the last time … oops, was that a speed bump? No, it was just a Honda Civic whose driver did not get far enough up on the sidewalk.

Tonight will be a great night. I will break out the Icy Hot and have me a big 'ol movie nap. I am such a rebel!

Loving Life

I have been pondering life a lot recently. I have come to realize that I don't understand it very much. One fall day forty-something years ago, I just kinda fell into this world and I fell like I am just supposed to keep busy for upwards of 100 years and then I will just kinda fall out. The trouble is that I am not really quite sure what I am supposed to be doing. Almost all of the advice on what you are supposed to do is simply opinions which have come from other people. Some religions have guidelines for living, but even those don't really say what I am supposed to do tomorrow. So, I tend to just make myself busy at the things I enjoy. I guess the hardest part to understand is why we put ourselves into positions to spend our lives doing things we do not enjoy. If the path of life is up to us, then why do we often choose to include the stuff we do not like. I know that some things we do not like are simply necessary, like taking out the garbage. But, why do people take a job that they hate when other jobs are clearly available. Or is it that they simply hate the job they take. Are some people just gonna hate any job, no matter what it is?

I know I am rambling. My thoughts are all over the place sometimes. The bottom line is that I love life and love living, but I am simply awfully curious as to how I got here and where I am going and what the heck is my purpose in the meantime?

Mowing and Blowing

I got to do my FAVORITE chore yesterday. I got to mow the grass. My yard is about 3/4 of an acre and has some banks and hills in it. It also has 14,329 trees and shrubs to mow around. Oh, and the riding mower finally died late last year and I have been putting off buying a new one. So, I got to push mow the yard yesterday. The push mower is also old. I actually started to mow last week. I had been at it for about 10 minutes when I had to stop to move some debris. When I got ready to start again, I pulled the starter cord and the rope broke. So, I got to be mower repairman that day. The next 3 days it rained ... a lot. Then the sun came out nice and warm. Grass LOVES that weather scenario. So, yesterday I was mowing thick, luscious, tall grass. The newly repaired mower did not like this scenario at all! It voiced its opinion by shutting itself off several times due to the strain. When that did not convince me, the mower took more drastic steps! I was coming up the hill by the side of the house when all of the sudden one of the front wheels just fell off! I kicked the mower and went into the house. So, today I get to play mower repairman again and then I get to mow the other half of the yard. Oh for joy!

Forward one day ...

At last the lawn is mowed. As previously stated, a cord broke and the wheel fell off, but yesterday I was a determined man. By the end of the ordeal, the mower was leaking oil and sputtering and spewing black smoke, and shutting down every five minutes, but I was determined that this mower was gonna mow the yard one last time even if I had to physically remove its blade and hack down the rest of the grass. I WON! I AM THE MAN!

This also reminds me of another event. A friend of mine was moving from a house to a condominium. He and his wife simply didn't enjoy having yard work and such to do ... maybe I need a condo too! He came to me and said he had some things to sell. You know how I love yard sales. Well, this was like a private screening! He was offering up a small garden tiller, a nice Craftsman pressure washer and a snowblower! He said his wife had bought them for him, but he had never used them. I gave him $160. What a bargain! Well, it was late summer, I tried the tiller. It was small but worked ok. The pressure washer seemed to be perfect. It was probably $300-$400 in the store. It was missing one hose but that was no problem. I couldn't try the snowblower in 80 degree weather but I was happy with the deal. Along came winter and in mid-December we got a good powdery eight inch snowfall. I thought, "Hey, it's time to pull out my other new toy!" As I had mentioned, the old owner had never used these items. The snowblower looked brand new. I filled it with fuel and fired it up and away I went. First trip down the drive went smoothly. I was throwing snow like a pro. I began my return trip and the directional lever that controls which way you throw the snow fell off. A minor inconvenience, but I was getting this job done in a flash. A couple more trips up the drive and the cable that connects to the drive and tells the blower to move became disconnected down near the motor. Next, the handle became all sort of wobbly. This machine was disintegrating right there in my hands! Again, I AM THE MAN! I WAS GOING TO WIN! I did finish the drive. I had to bend over the whole time and pull the drive cable while steering with my knee and moving the directional thingy with my elbow, but I WON! I think shoveling may have been easier, but I won!

Petty Things

I do not watch a lot of TV. I am simply too busy. I do like to turn it on for a few minutes when I go to bed just to unwind a bit. Yesterday evening it was approaching bedtime and I was curious about the weather, so I flipped on the TV for a minute. While changing channels, I came across a show by Stephen Hawking about the universe and all that sort of stuff. I became engrossed in the subject matter and sat down to take it all in. He talked about the different theories on origins of the universe and how there could be multiple universes and other dimensions and how there are so many things we simply do not know or understand. He dwelled quite a bit on black holes and how there are massive black holes at the center of each galaxy slowly sucking in all that surrounds them. He talked about how we do not know what really is going on inside of that black hole, but that it was a big key to understanding this universe we live in. For me, it was a fascinating show.

The bad thing is that I am left with the feeling that I am a spec of dust. I am merely a spec in relation to the size of the earth. The earth is a spec in relation to the sun. The sun is truly a small spec amongst all of the other stars out there. And our galaxy is just one of countless galaxies in our universe. And it is theorized that there could be billions of other universes. Now that makes me a spec! Not to mention the fact that he said that when the Earth gets swallowed by a black hole, it will be squeezed down to the size of a pea! Just how big will that make me!

So for today, I feel pretty insignificant and humbled. It really makes me look at the petty things I typically worry about in a whole new light and perhaps that is a good thing.

Live a Little

I find that there are simply not enough entertaining TV shows these days. We all have like a million channels, but nothing worthwhile to watch. Still, that does not seem to stop many people from spending literally hours every day staring at the TV screen. I therefore started to calculate my own television watching time. I sometimes will watch a whole ballgame or a whole movie (contrary to popular belief, I do not sleep through every one of them) and yet some days I watch little or no TV at all. So, I calculated my average to be about an hour a day.

I will now wait while you calculate YOUR average ... go ahead, I am waiting ... doo bee doo dum dum ... don't forget to carry the one ... dee boo deeb deeb doo ... done yet? ... OK!

Now remember that number I told you not to forget? You don't listen very well do you? Go ahead and peek back up to the top of the story. There you go! 1440! Take the number of minutes you watch TV in a day (if yours was hours, then convert it to minutes first) ... again, take that number of minutes you watch TV in a day and divide it by 1440. 1440 is the total number of minutes in a day. For instance, in my case, I watch 60 minutes per day divided by 1440 = .04166666, or rounded = 4.2% of my day is spent in front of a TV. Now, I decided to calculate the average life at 75 years. Myself, of course, I plan on being around for at least double that. But, for these calculations, I went conservative. So, if I take 75 years and multiply by .042 (4.2% or in your case whatever your percentage was) I come up with 3.15. That means I will spend approximately 3 years and two months of my preciously short life staring at a television screen! I know that there are people who spend much more time watching than me. I am certain that some will spend 10 years there! Amazing!

As for me, I will still watch things I consider to be quality time spent, but I am going to spend much more of that idle TV time actually living my own life from now on!

Keys

I can't find the keys to the Jeep. I used to be able to just go to the drawer and get one of the four spare ones. But then, over time, my two daughters started driving it and together with Sally, they have lost all of my spares. Me? No, of course I have not lost any of them! I am only responsible for sometimes, on rare occasions, temporarily misplacing or more likely accidentally dropping the main key somewhere, usually while I am in the middle of some sort of hard work or very important project. I am not the one who just all willy nilly forgets where I threw it down carelessly. Am I ever going to get these women properly trained?

Anyhow, here I sit with no key. I am supposed to go get blood drawn this morning for those annual tests they like to do to see if I am gonna hang around another year or not. I am not supposed to eat before this test. And, yes I am kinda cranky about that. I am hungry and yet I do not want to eat because I am certain that I will find where my key accidentally fell out of my pocket at any moment now and therefore I will be able to go get this blood test out of the way. And since these women in my life have made this such a traumatic experience by so carelessly losing all of my spares,

I will probably have to reward/console myself after the blood test with a stop at the pancake palace to replenish my system. Keep me in your thoughts and prayers!

My Prescription

I have a sinus infection. I feel like crud and I need the whole world to feel sorry for me. I have no energy. All I want to do is lay around. I am sleeping a lot. I went to the doctor and he gave me drugs. I am just waiting on the recovery to commence.

Why should you feel sorry for me? Well, I am a man and I am sick. What? Is that not enough of a reason? Well, ok, Sally refuses to take care of me. She says I am a big boy and can take care of myself. Does she not hear me say that I am sick? ... and a man? She tells me I can get my own tissue and make my own soup and to not yell for her just because my pillow needs fluffing. I bet you are feeling sorry for me now! Heck, I even offered to have her run to the store and buy me one of those little bells so that I could just give her a jingle when I needed her. She just doesn't understand.

Another thing that is strange about being sick is the doctor's prescription for me. He gave me an antibiotic to take. That is pretty normal. But, he also told me to put Vick's Vapor Rub on the bottoms of my feet and then go to bed. Somehow he thinks my feet will cure my head. I am thinking maybe he needs something to cure his head. I must admit that is does feel good. But the biggest benefit is that mean, old, uncaring Sally hates the smell of the stuff.

Where's My Beef?

I am hungry. It is nearly noon and I have not taken the time to eat yet today. Well, I did have a bowl of cereal and a potato chip, but those don't count. What I mean is that I am ready for a meal. I looked in the cabinet and the refrigerator but found nothing of interest. It is amazing to me how these places can be full and yet there is nothing there to eat.

The problem is that Sally did the grocery shopping recently. She needs some better guidance in this area. For instance, she did buy canned spaghetti's, which is a good choice. But, she got the ones with no little meatballs or hotdogs in them! Now, who in the world wants to eat that? She is always buying food that is missing something. She says she is simply trying to eliminate excess fat and carbs from out diets. I tell her that I am a growing boy and I need my fats and carbs. She says that is part of the problem. I am growing in all of the wrong directions.

I have tried to explain to her that bringing a salad to the dinner table is fine, but she needs to follow it up with a big hunk of something more substantial. She does not understand that a baked potato is meant as a compliment and not as a centerpiece of the meal. And who the heck needs broccoli steamed with nothing on it more than once in a lifetime? Sally seems to think that three or four times per week you need to have something plain and green. She seems to have a prejudice against the colors of brown and white being on your plate. She wants all yellows and oranges and greens and stuff. Those are fine for small sides, but the main course is missing from most of her meals.

It is a good thing that I stand up for myself. If not, I would simply wither up and blow away and it would be all Sally's fault.

The House That Built Me

I was recently driving along listening to the radio when a song by the singer Miranda Lambert came on. It is called "The House That Built Me." The song title got me to thinking about the house that built ME! Yep it is still standing. My mother still lives in it. She and my father moved there in about 1954. It is nothing fancy and nothing large, but it will always be home. I know all of the nooks and crannies which I explored growing up. They are all quite vivid in my memory. I know about certain little hidden marks where I tracked my growth and special hiding places for things I wanted to keep from my brother. I could walk in right now to my old room and open the bottom right drawer of my desk and there is a plastic baggie containing a sand dollar I collected on a field trip with my high school science teacher. Boy was she cute! ... oh, I guess that should be another story ... Anyhow, this old house is where I learned to walk and talk. This is the poor house that endured my early days as a drummer. This place has seen almost all of the most important people in my life pass through its doors. The place is just bursting with memories both good and bad from the past 47 years.

The yard upon which the house sits is also a large part of my past. It is where I spent my nearly endless summers exploring and where I barreled down the hill on all sorts of sleds in the winter. It is the place I played tag and baseball. It is also where I buried just about every pet I have ever had. There are two rows of pine trees lining the walkway down the hill to the garage. There must have originally been about a dozen of them. Two of them died. One was replaced by a blue spruce. It was my favorite even though it really didn't match all of the green ones. Maybe that was why I liked it because it was different like me! The other dead one was replaced by me. I brought home a seedling from school on Arbor day. Dad thought that was the perfect spot for it. I would always run down the hill and hurdle that tree on my way to the garage. My children now think I am telling a tall tale considering that the little tree that I planted is now probably forty feet tall! Along the very top of the yard was a woods. I used to gather hickory nuts up there. There was also a drainage ditch along the one edge. Me and the neighbor kid used to argue about which of our families actually owned the ditch. Of course we all know it was mine! The old bush where Goldie hid from another neighbor's vicious dog to keep from getting eaten is still there too. Tons of memories. It is indeed the place that helped to build me.

These days people move so often that many of us cannot identify home the way that I can. For me it is a small three bedroom on a bank above the road on the outskirts of a country village. It is a collection of sticks and mortar that makes up the place where so much of my life has happened. I feel reconnected with me every time that I visit.

The down side is that I do worry about what will happen to that old house. I have had the luxury of always being able to just walk in the door and sit down. There may come a day in the future when that may not be possible and that does sadden me a bit. I don't ever want to feel like I cannot go home.

Growth Spurt

I must be going through a growth spurt. I feel like I am getting taller. I feel it every time I bend over to pick something up. The floor is getting further away all the time! I have not measured myself in many years, but I surely must be approaching 6'6." Ten years ago I was about 5'11", but I just know that floor is much farther away now! It is a really long way down there!.

Sally says I am just plain crazy. She says that I am growing for sure, but in all of the wrong directions. She has this crazy idea that I am simply getting older and therefore it is much more difficult for me to bend all the way down to the floor. I think she is just plain crazy herself! She is just jealous of all the pretty girls looking at her handsome, tall husband! That's what I think!

I would prove to her that I am taller if I could only remember where I put that darned yardstick. Sally says that is another sign of my aging. She says I am forgetful and that I tell her the same stories over and over again. She obviously has no idea what she is talking about. Did I mention that I think I am growing taller?

Even More Yard Sale Mania

As I have mentioned before, I love going to yard sales. I love snooping for hidden treasures amongst other people's junk. I buy all sorts of stuff. Yes, I am a bit of a pack rat. But only of valuable stuff.

Sally seems to disagree with me as to what the word valuable actually means. But, I am good at spotting a bargain when I see it. She would be having a yard sale of her own to rid our home of some of my most valuable treasures if I weren't keeping a very close eye on her. That weather barometer out in the garage is gonna look wonderful on the wall next to the front door someday, as soon as I fix the frame on it. I also have a whole box of computer power cords that I bought for $5. Heck, one cord is worth that much and you never know when you might have a need for one. And a guy can never have too many Bathroom Readers. Electronic gadgets? Well, most of them just need a little TLC when I get around to it and then they will be good as new. Bicycles? I would hate for some kid to come along and not have a bike and me not have a spare one in the garage for them. Tools? Now really! It is impossible to have too many screwdrivers and socket wrenches, just impossible, I tell you!

Much to Sally's dismay, our youngest child, Joannie, also loves the garage sales. She enjoys trodding along with me through countless communities until the car simply cannot hold anymore stuff. Joannie seems to find something at each and every sale that she simply MUST have. It is amazing how deprived this child is. I never would have dreamed that she needed so many things. One thing that Joannie does share with Sally is the opinion that many of MY purchases are simply insanity. She simply does not see the value in my choices. Why buy a pair of stereo speakers when there are perfectly good Barbie dolls there for the taking? Well, I am here to tell you that I have had the last laugh this time by golly!

This past Saturday Sally and Evelyn joined Joannie and I for a couple of hours of yard sale heaven. It was great weather, there were tons of sales, and Joannie and I both had some spending money. I bought several interesting artifacts, but one purchase in particular was especially troubling to Joannie.

"Why would you buy that big box of records when you don't even have a record player?", she asked.

I tried to explain to her that on rare occasions there will be a highly valuable and collectible record in a box like this. Obviously, she was not impressed with this logic, because she told everyone she knew about my "dumb" purchase of a box of records with no way to play them all weekend long ... At least until Sunday evening ...

You see, Sunday evening I had some time to start going through my "dumb" box of records. In it I found a Disney soundtrack from the 1950's which was worth about $50. Not bad for a $5 box of "dumb records." But wait, there's more! Contained in this box of "dumb" records was a boxed set of 7 Beethoven albums. I looked it up on the internet and found that this item was of little value. Out of curiosity, however, I decided to open it up and peek inside.

I opened it to find that there were only two of the seven records in there. The extra space, however, had been filled with a bunch of little boxes and cases and envelopes, each of which was filled with uncirculated coin proof sets! So much for my "dumb box of records"! Joannie now was all about sharing in my wonderful find! I told her to go play with her "dumb" Barbie dolls!

I would have been inclined to return the coins to the people I bought the records from, but we went to so many yard sales that I would have had no idea where I even got them. I am betting that from now on Sally and Joannie won't be so quick to judge my wise and wonderful purchases so harshly. Who's the big dog now?

That's My Boy

Will came to me last night and handed me a "Certificate of Academic Achievement."

"What's this for?" I asked.

"I don't know." he replied, "They just called me up to the office and gave it to me."

That's my boy! Rewarded for just kinda being there! Will is just a happy-go-lucky kinda 15 year old. To him, school is just something he has to do between video games and computers and hanging out with friends and family. Rarely is he not smiling. He seems to be a truly happy kid who wants to remain a kid. He shows no desire to ever grow up. I am very happy that he enjoys where he is in life. So many kids are in such a hurry to be grownups. Where is the fun in that?

If Will is making good grades and it is not really a priority to know why they are honoring him with a certificate, then I am ok with that. He is succeeding at being Will and that is all that really matters.

Mean Old Mom

I was talking to dear old mom over the weekend. The first thing you have to understand is that mom does not mince words. She just says what she feels. We were having just our typical conversation about the weather and which kid was working what shift today and what was for dinner … you know, the normal stuff. Then, we got off on the subject of how she wants her tombstone turned around because she thinks it faces the wrong direction, but when she does that she will have to have it re-engraved because my dad's and her names would be backwards. She stated this would be quite expensive. I suggested that we just put arrows on there pointing toward the right direction where each one is planted. She seemed to think that she would be the joke of the whole graveyard if I did that. All of the other dead people would be making fun of her. I still thought it was a brilliant idea.

It was then that the conversation turned ugly. She said, "You'd better start thinking about a will and where you will be buried too. You ain't no spring chicken you know!" And I thought my mommy loved me! I don't even know yet what I want to be when I grow up and she is already suggesting that my impending demise may be right around the corner! And to suggest that I am getting old! Well, I am here to tell you that there is still lots of spring in my chicken! So take that mommy! Stuff that in your pie hole! Oh, and by the way, could you send me some of your homemade sugar cookies soon? I am running a bit low.

An older gentleman and I were talking about happiness and we both agreed that being content and thankful for what you have is the key to happiness. Being in a constant state of unfulfilled want is the source of many a misery.

Spoiled Pets

We have four cats. Two of them love being outdoors and love the sense of adventure of exploring the big, exciting world of our yard. All of those bushes and trees and weeds and tall grasses (another reason not to mow so often). They love to eye up birds and squirrels and bugs as possible prey ... not that these two have ever caught anything. The other two cats, however, view the outdoors as some sort of punishment. If you head towards them and they think you are gonna take them out, they will make a mad dash for the bedroom or a nearby closet. If you do round them up and put them out, they do nothing but complain. The one seems annoyed by the lack of climate control and soft comforters. The other constantly looks around as if he is sure something is about to jump right out of a bush and try to eat him. If you were to drop these two in a woods, they would just starve to death. The other two would just be happy as could be ... well at least until it rained or something. The pets we care for have become almost as spoiled as we humans are. Many of us would be quite upset without central heat and air conditioning or if we had to go out and hunt down our food somewhere other than the grocery store. Heaven forbid if we had to go outside to use the bathroom when it was below zero.

Seasons

It feels like Summer outside today. The sweat is a flowin' from the brows of anyone out there for very long. I understand that most people love summertime weather. For me, it is just ok. I much prefer the Fall. I like cool mornings and warmish afternoons. In the summer, the heat can often be downright uncomfortable, leaving us to run and hide in our air conditioned houses. I would prefer to have the days when you can turn off the AC and open the windows. On those days, when evening comes, you can curl up under a blanket on the couch and feel just about perfect.

Overall, I enjoy all of the seasons for different reasons. Summer is great for playing Frisbee with the kids in the evening or for making corn and potatoes and sausages on the grill. Fall is best for the beauty of nature and the wonderful crispness in the air. It is when I feel most alive. Winter is a great time to "hole up" with family and friends around a warm fire to watch a movie after being outside sledding in the snow all afternoon. Spring for me is about rebirth, new beginnings and the coming to life of all that is around me. So, while I may complain or show favoritism, each season carries its own blessings for me.

Cherry Juice

As I am writing this, I am hungry and that got me to thinking. I know that this whole thinking thing is usually where all of my trouble starts. Anyhow, I got to thinking about what to have to eat and I had an epiphany. I realized that just about everything we drink, with the exception of water, is sweet! We eat foods that are sweet or salty or bitter or sour etc.. But, when was the last time you had a salty drink? I know, I know, sometimes they put salt on the glass on some mixed drinks, but when did you have a salty drink that was not sweet too? Well, come to think of it, I have drunk pickle juice a time or two, but I try to refrain from doing that daily. And how about sour? Lemons are sour, but we make sweet lemonade with them and grapefruits are kinda sour, but with a natural sweetness in there. I did see something or read something about how good cherry juice was for you one time a while back. You were supposed to drink it in its natural form. It was supposed to help with some ailment I was having or something. It was difficult to come by, but I finally found some in the health foods section of a store I went to. It was "all natural unsweetened cherry juice." I got home and poured me a big 'ol glass. How bad could it be? I love cherry Kool-Aid. So, I took a big snort of it. I quickly learned what it feels like to have your lips curled up inside of your eyelids. WOW! Of course, the next thing I did was test it out on Sally and the kids one at a time. That juice may not have cured whatever was ailing me, but it sure was worth the entertainment value I got out of watching the rest of the family try it.

ME Day

It is late in the evening and I am very tired. My day started about 5am and I have been going strong ever since. It is now 12:24am. Nineteen hours of nonstop living. I have not had time to sit and loaf or to watch TV or to take a nap or just do something relaxing. I have been on the go all day. How did my life get so busy? I am not that important! I am barely worthy of being called a regular guy. Yet my life is full of commitments and demands on my time. I need a ME day!

Let's see, for my ME day I will first go to bed at 8:00pm the night before so that I will be well rested. I will awaken without the help of an alarm or a kid tugging at me. I will just slowly come alive around 7:30am. Sally will have breakfast waiting (Hey this is MY day, not hers!), some scrambled eggs with spicy mustard in them and some French toast with real maple syrup and crispy bacon. I will read the paper while consuming my morning meal. I will then head out to my 9:00 tee time on this bright, sunny, 70 degree morning to go golfing with a couple of friends. They will be good golfers, but just a little off on their game today while I seem to be playing the best of my life. At the clubhouse after the first nine holes, I will grab a hot dog and some fries to eat along the way. After the golf game, I will meet Sally for lunch at 1:00 at that Mexican joint. Boy! There is a lot of food in MY day! We will then go for a bike ride through the country during the afternoon. When I arrive home, the kids will all be up for a game of wiffle ball. I rock at wiffle ball! Then we will break out the Frisbee and maybe even the Bocce Balls. I will then end my day curled up with a good book of trivia and some Earl Grey Tea. Well, there is my day! Great to dream anyhow, and besides, even my relaxing day sounds awfully busy!

Riding in Style

I finally broke down and bought a new riding mower. I hated to do it, but Sally rejected my ideas of a goat or a couple of sheep or declaring the backyard a wildlife sanctuary. Hey, I was just trying to help all of those squirrels and raccoons and ducks and deer who like to come by for a visit from time to time. I am just a selfless guy like that. Sally thinks I was just being lazy. I think I was being proactive.

So, anyhow, Sally said she did not care which tractor I bought, as long as I came home with one, and not one from a garage sale either! (She is always foiling my plans like that)

I went to the store. I talked to the sales guy. I got the scoop on all of the different models. I made my selection. I held out for a great deal. I made myself appear just interested enough to MAYBE buy one, without appearing desperate enough to NEED one. This kept the sales guy offering me stuff. I ended up getting a lower price, a free wagon, free delivery and the guy is going to come over and mow my yard three or four times to make sure everything goes ok. Well, I got all but the last one, although I did lobby for him to do that.

I was proud of myself! With the free delivery, I decided to go ahead and purchase a few other items that I needed since they would go ahead and bring them at the same time for no charge! I had mastered the art of the deal! Sally was gonna be so proud!

So, the next morning the delivery truck arrives and brings me all of my goodies. Sally takes one look and says, "I don't particularly like the color. Why didn't you get one of those green ones?" I swear I can never win with that girl.

Grilled

Tonight I am cooking on the grill. I am making steaks and chicken and bratwurst and hot dogs and potatoes and corn on the cob. It is a pretty cool summer activity. What I have been pondering, however, is why is it that grill cooking is considered a man's job? Don't get me wrong, I enjoy grilling. I am just curious how this practice came about. It is true that times are changing, but in traditional roles, the woman did all of the cooking inside the house, yet the moment you took the food outside, the man was supposed to know what to do with it. Where did that idea come from? Jim can't fry his own egg, but he is supposed to go out and handle the ribs and chops with ease over an open fire.

Now, to a totally different subject. As I am sitting here writing, the second toe on each foot, you know, the one beside the big toe, just decided to go to sleep. Not numb, just that pins and needles thing. The whole episode lasted about two minutes. I am curious how these two toes on opposite feet communicated and decided to take a nap at the same time. All of the other eight toes stayed on the job, just those two acted funny. I suppose I was doing something to irritate a nerve in my back or something to cause this, but it is still just odd. When you think about it, little odd "episodes" happen in our bodies daily. We all have pains or sensations for which we have no explanation. We just assume they are benign and go on. It is true that they usually are benign, but I remain curious as to what they are. For instance, at this very moment, taking inventory of my body, I feel four little itchy spots, two pain spots and two tingling spots. None of these are significant, but they are there. One pain spot is sinus related and minor. One is in my hip area because the pants I am wearing have shrunk just a bit around the waist. Do you have that problem too? All of my pants seem to be shrinking these days. I just don't understand. I have an itchy spot on the inside of my elbow. There is nothing there, it just itches. Anyhow, I am just curious what causes all of this stuff. Try it for yourself. Sit back right now and take inventory of all of the sensations that you are experiencing right now. Freaky huh?

"Sally! There's something wrong with me. Two of my toes just died! I need you to do the grilling tonight!"

Wisdom

I have been pondering what I have learned so far in life. I am supposed to be gaining some wisdom along the way. Boy, the world is in trouble if all of the wisdom is supposed to come from people like me. I have lots of opinions, but they are merely that. So, with that said, here are my opinions that I have come up with.

- Never marry someone thinking they can change (we've all heard that one), but also never marry someone thinking they can change you.
- Always be yourself. Be true to who you are. If you don't, you are only hurting yourself and those who think they know you.
- Practice kindness every day. The rewards that will come back to you are priceless.
- Don't eat radishes after 6pm once you reach the age of 40 … or pizza or tacos or …
- Share all that you have because you do not truly own any of it. We are just temporary renters of everything here on Earth.

- Invest heavily in friendships and relationships
- Cook at home. Not only does it taste better and is often healthier, it develops family time when you involve the kids … and heck, this way they will learn something that will keep them from starving to death when they get older.
- Don't stay mad. Get over it and move on. Life is moving forward and so should you.
- Wrestle with the dog at least a couple of times a month. It is good for the both of you.
- Don't be afraid to play at any age. Get right out there with the kids and have a blast.
- Experience something new and different regularly.
- Don't be cruel to other living things.
- Now is the greatest time. It is the only time you will ever possess. Make the most of it.

Tonight was fish for dinner. I enjoy baked fish and most of the kids like it well enough too. The problem is that the cats give me fits all night long on fish night. They smell that aroma in the air and become the most loving creatures you have ever seen. It is almost as bad as boiled catnip night!

Fee Me

I have been a bit overwhelmed by life the past several days. Sometimes that just happens. Something will come up out of the blue and just change all of your plans. Anyhow, all you can do is adjust and move forward.

Something that has been bugging me recently is fees. Fees have become the sneaky way of stealing extra money from my wallet. I have 3 different debit cards. If I want to withdraw my own money and am not near a machine owned by my own bank, someone wants a fee for the convenience. Ok, I can accept the concept. The trouble is that if I only want $20, the fee can be as high as $3. That is a significant percentage. Still, that is a choice I make. The one debit card even charges a fee each time I call and check to see how much money I have in my account. The fees I get most upset about are the ones charged by utilities for paying my bill. No matter which payment method I use, the one utility charges $5.95 for the right to pay my bill. Of course I have the right to NOT pay my bill and then be charged a different fee.

I sold something on Ebay recently. They charged me a fee to list the item, another fee based upon the final selling price and then Paypal (owned by Ebay) charged me a fee for collecting the money for me. I would have been fine if the buyer sent me a money order or cash, but Ebay did not allow that. I think it was because there was no fee involved. So, in the end, I made next to nothing for the sale.

I think I am gonna start charging my own fees. Let's see, how about a junk mail processing fee? I can charge the garbage man a fee for not returning the garbage cans to their proper location. I feel I deserve a fee for needing to remain on hold longer than 2 minutes when I call a company for service. How about a waiting in line fee for the stores who intentionally hire too few cashiers? I can charge a processing fee to telemarketers for the right to speak with me during dinner. I believe I have hit upon a gold mine! I will be busy the rest of today making my new fee schedule!

Dad's Day

It's Father's Day. I was awakened an hour ago to breakfast in bed prepared by nine year old Joannie. It was the best Honey Combs and orange juice I ever had. I am sure there will be many other moments for me to enjoy today. I will have a great time just being with my kids.

I really think that the name of today should be changed. It should be Dad's Day. Anybody can be a father, but being a dad is what should be honored. It is not simply because I am one, but because being a dad means being there every day to do all of the little stuff, the important stuff that helps a child to find themselves and reach their own potential in life. A dad is a guidepost and a crutch to lean upon when needed. A dad is someone you know will always have your back when you are right, but will always tell you when you are wrong and still be right there to catch you and break your fall.

My dad passed away nearly five years ago. He was all of those things. If I ever become half the man he was, I will be doing alright. Hardly a day goes by that I do not reflect upon the things I learned from him in making decisions in my own life. I often do not even think about it. It is just a part of who I am and what makes me. Yet sometimes I do look at a situation and think about how he would have handled it. I do not always follow the same path that he would have, although I would probably be better off if I did.

So today I will enjoy the attention and the love shown to me and I will try not to take for granted the long term effect I may be having on my own children. While I will long for just one more day with my dad, I will cherish one more day of being one to my kids.

Happy Dad's Day!

Mrs. P's

I had an errand to run this morning to an "artsy" section of town. You know, the kind of area where there seems to be a collection of shops that would appeal to hippies both old and new. There is a clothing store where you can buy 40 year old shirts and a health food store and lots of places selling crafts. Anyhow, just down the street a ways is a bread store I have always wanted to check out. It is a place that makes fresh, from scratch, no preservative breads of many varieties. There were three customers in line in front of me and all appeared to be regulars. One had called in advance to reserve his order and another had driven sixty miles just to buy his bread here. I gathered from the conversation that he made this trip every week or two. The shop was quite simple. There was a menu of what would be available each day of the week and the shelves behind the counter were lined with a variety of fresh loaves. I would guess there were about 20 different choices there. They also had a couple of kinds of rolls and even homemade hot dog buns. It was an interesting little joint.

I made my selection of two loaves and made my way home with my bounty. When I got home, I opened up one loaf and took out the heel (the best part of homemade bread) and slathered on some jelly. It was very good. Crusty on the outside and soft/fresh in the middle. Just what good bread should be.

It made me reminisce about the best bread I have ever eaten. It was made by a little old woman named Mrs. P. She had this jar of stuff she called starter. She would use out of it but never use it all. It was a liquid to which she would add yeast and sugar to keep it "growing." Every loaf of bread she ever made come from this mixture. Her bread was so incredible that you required nothing else with it to enjoy it. No need for butter or jelly or peanut butter or anything else. It was at its absolute best if simply left to stand alone. It was one of those pure food pleasures I will probably never get to enjoy again.

I will enjoy my breads I got today and will probably return to buy more. I may even become a regular. Yet, as good as this bread is, it will only leave me longing for a mere morsel of Mrs. P.'s

Diary of a Stroke

About three weeks ago I came downstairs to my computer, sat down to log onto the internet and discovered that my right hand would not do the tasks I was asking it to do. It was not obeying my commands as usual. It was acting with a mind of its own. My hand simply felt clumsy or "off." I decided to just chalk it up to old age and go to bed. The next morning my hand still did not seem just right, but I really paid little attention to it until I attempted to open a bottle of soda pop and was completely unable to get a firm enough grip on it to budge the lid. Something was definitely different.

I decided to call my family doctor. He said, "Well, to be safe, come in and see me."

So, off to the doctor I went. He checked me over and said I looked healthy and "presented well." All of my stats were good. He was guessing I had a pinched nerve. He also said he was really on the fence about sending me to have a test done just as a precaution. Finally, he said that if he had to debate about it that long that he should just go ahead and have me do the test. The test was an MRI of my brain. The only MRI I had ever encountered was a look into my shoulder a few years ago. It was done in an open

MRI machine. This time it was to be done at a local hospital in a closed unit. I am really not claustrophobic, so I did not have much concern. I even had less concern when they asked if I wanted to watch ESPN using some TV goggles while I was being tested. For me, the biggest issue was laying still for that long. I am a kind of antsy person by nature.

The next morning my doctor called and said, "I got your MRI results and I am shocked. The test shows that you may have had a stroke."

A wave of hot, tingling, ugly nervous energy just rolled through my body. What could this mean? Was I on the verge of something horrible or was this just a minor hiccup? I am by all accounts a very healthy 47 year old man. Was that perception about to change? I asked the doctor how seriously I should take this and he said that doing further testing was crucial to determine whether this was a one time thing or something more ominous. He had my attention. Now every little oddity I felt was a magnified reason to sort of hold my breath and brace for this unknown monster to attack again. It was about 3 days until I was sitting face to face with a neurologist and while my hand function was improving, my nerves were just about to jump out of my skin. The unknown is a horrible thing.

The neurologist was surely going to tell me this was no big deal. Just go on with my life, right? Well, here is the general conversation as he gave it to me … "I looked at your MRI scan and there was a shadow in one spot. I would not necessarily agree with the initial diagnosis of a stroke (alright! Good Neurologist! Tell me that good news!) It is possible, but I would be more likely to consider this an area of concern for MS, Multiple Sclerosis (Now, wait a minute! You tell me the good news about the stroke diagnosis and then turn right around and burst my bubble with MS! Bad Neurologist! Bad Bad!).

He then went on to say his second choice would be a seizure disorder and thirdly an infection of unknown origins in the brain (So much for thinking he was Mr. Wonderful!). He prescribed that I have every test known to man over the coming days to get a better idea what was going on.

The first foray into this whole testing phase was blood work. Two vials, two minutes, no sweat. The next day was a Video EEG. They hooked up about 20 electrodes to my head then shut me in a room for four hours while they observed my via closed circuit television. I was allowed to eat, read, sleep or watch tv in my cage. I now know how a zoo animal feels. When the four hours was up, I was very much ready to get out of that place. So the next morning, guess what? I got to do the 4 hour video EEG Again!!!! WEEEEEHAW-WWWWWWWWWW! If I wasn't crazy before, well ...

It gets better. On this day not only did I get to be confined like a prisoner in county lockup for half the day, this time they put the electrodes on my head with some sort of head glue and sent me home with them on for the weekend. Have you ever gone into a bank or grocery store with twenty colorful wires protruding from your head all plugged into an electronic device strapped to your waist? I looked like a suicide bomber.

The weekend was interesting. I went to a few yard sales and for a couple of walks. People were staring at me like I was Lady Gaga. Sleeping was also a bit of a challenge, but I survived. These people weren't gonna break me that easily.

On the day following my lovely weekend, I was sent for an ultrasound of the blood vessels in my neck. That was cool. It was like a deep tissue massage. Maybe this whole testing thing was on the upswing.

Little did I know that the next trick up their sleeves was even more sinister than the EEG stuff. The doctor walks in and says,

"I am just gonna do a little nerve test here on your arms. It is called an ENG."

OK, Doc, three more little letters are not gonna break me. He took this little plastic bar with 3 little metal dots and taped it on my arm near my wrist. He then took some measurements. Finally, he placed this probe against my forearm and ZAP! This diabolical monster was now trying to electrocute me! I bet he zapped me twenty times. Then for good measure, he pulled out this long, skinny needle and pricked me with it three times in each arm. I think he did that just for the sheer pleasure of it.

I am supposedly all finished with my testing now. I am bothered by the fact that they keep all of the results a secret until my "follow-up appointment." It is this coming Thursday. I have no clue what they may have found and of course I hope for something simple. But either way, my life has been,, is and will probably continue to be a good one.

The Waiting

Well, after three weeks of medical tests and uncertainty, tomorrow is results day. It has been an interesting journey, to say the least. Now I will walk into the doctor's office and he will deliver the news. It could be good, bad, inconclusive or simply an unknown. Based upon my previous experiences with others having medical testing, I am betting on either inconclusive or unknown. We know a lot with technology, yet we don't know even more. No matter what the tests have to say, it is likely that my life will simply move forward and continue pretty much as normal. There is a small chance of something more earth-shattering, but most likely whatever I find out will not change my life on Friday or next week or next month.

The worst part has been the wait. The unknown is always the hardest. It creates much frustration. If there is some big news, I will simply do my best to make the best of it. No matter what the news, I have refocused on what truly matters in my life. It is time and people. Spending quality moments with those who mean the most to me. Good news or bad, that is what I will take from this experience.

Prescribed Loafing

I had my long awaited doctor's appointment today. The results were "inconclusive." He was, however, able to tell me that many of the worst case scenarios are a low probability. He said he is hoping that my leftover symptoms from whatever happened will simply subside with time. In the meantime, he wants me to loaf. Heck, I am an expert at that! Now I just need to convince Sally that I am simply doing it for the health benefits. Doctor's orders! Actually, I am not that good at plain old loafing, but I am good at tinkering, so that is probably what I will do more than loafing. They key to good tinkering is to never finish the projects you start … at least not for an extended period of time. You want to always have several things "in progress" so that you can justify choosing what you want to tinker on today. I come from a long line of very good tinkerers and I need to uphold the tradition.

Sally is not at all happy with the situation. I think she just knows that I will be around the house a lot more to bug her. Or maybe she is just upset that she now has to put on hold the plans she had made for my going away party. She did seem pretty excited about that for awhile. I am beginning to wonder if she was already shopping for my replacement. She would probably be smart to trade me in on a new model. One that makes more money or likes to mow the grass more often or never forgets to take the trash to the street on Sunday night.

In all honesty, she is a lucky girl to have me. I have handsomer disease and I get it more with each passing day. I am a wonderful provider. I provide dirty clothes and dirty dishes to keep her life fulfilled daily. I can cook! I provide lots of dirty dishes as well as dirty counters and floors and more when I cook. I tinker on the old fluffy dog's haircuts. Just look at the money I am saving! I always bring her gifts from the yard sales I visit. I don't snore as loud as she does. I could go on and on …

Un-Holiday

July the 5th 2010. What makes this day so special? It was a holiday. Oh so you say I am wrong? No, for many Americans Monday July 5, 2010 was a holiday. Since the 4th fell on a Sunday, many people had Monday off from work in its place. Many businesses were closed and it was just like a real holiday. In my opinion these "unholiday" holidays make the best kind. The real holidays are so packed full of stuff and business to be taken care of, whereas these unholidays are mostly just free time.

Take me for example. On the 4th I had to go to the grocery store. I bought $200 worth of food and waited in a line ten deep to just check out. Out of 15 lanes, only three were open, probably due to people calling in "sick." You would think management would figure this out or maybe they simply don't care that I spent 30 minutes standing there reading the Enquirer. By the way, you would never believe who had plastic surgery and how they are hiding a deep dark secret about how it turned out ruining their relationship with the father of their hidden lovechild who was recently abducted by aliens and subjected to unimaginable medical testing.

Anyhow, so I get back from the grocery and Sally is now pacing the floor waiting for me to get home so that we could take a passel of children to the parade so they could chase candy being thrown from passing floats in 90+ degree heat and also see my daughter march past playing saxophone in the school band for 30 seconds.

Next, upon arriving home, I started preparing the feast for the evening. I grilled for 3 and one half hours! Potatoes and corn and steaks and hamburgers and hot dogs and bratwurst and chicken and that pesky little dog from across the street and ... well, you get the picture. Of course there were side items to prepare as well. I fed approximately 14 people a feast fit for a king. Then it was time to load up the car and head to the fireworks show. Again, horrible traffic jam and whining, tired kids.

The last thing on the agenda after finally arriving back home at 1130pm, was to set off our own little batch of fireworks. I am sure the neighbors appreciated all of the entertainment at midnight. Of course they have come to expect it. One lady actually came over when we first moved in and thanked us by saying she was happy that they were no longer considered the weird family in the neighborhood.

Ok, so that was my July 4th. What did I do on July 5th? I went to see the movie "Toy Story 3" in the afternoon. Other than that, it was an uneventful day. That is what I call a holiday!

Introspection

Why am I here? This is an existential question that everyone asks at one time or another. People come up with all sorts of answers about their calling in life or the reasons for their presence. Many ideas are very haughty taughty or of high moral standards. Some are just downright unusual.

I have started to understand that my personal reason for existing is very different depending upon who you would ask. To the dogs, I am a source of food. To the cats, I am a source of food and a big pillow. To the kids, I am a source of food and an ATM and a taxi driver. To my wife Sally, I am a source of frustration. She keeps trying unsuccessfully to train me properly in chore completion and proper etiquette in public. It is a losing battle for her on both fronts.

To the people who read my books and my blog, I am hopefully a source of entertainment. To friends, I am a source of fear that they may become the next chapter in one of my books. This list could go on and on! I am a lot of things to a lot of people. Every person in this world has significance and importance. It is good to recognize your own self worth in the world from time to time.

Payday

One of the best memories of growing up for me was the biweekly Friday trip to town. That was my dad's payday and so as soon as he got home from work, we would be on our way 15 miles down Highway 21 to the "city." It was a city of maybe 4,000 people. That was huge compared to my village of 200. The trip always included a stop at the grocery store and the bank, but it also nearly always included a stop at G. C .Murphy. G. C. Murphy was what was called a five and dime store or simply a five and ten. It was three stories of dime store heaven and they had everything from clothes to household items to hardware and tools to records and toys. I loved that place! It was the kind of place where you could browse the latest offerings by the Doobie Brothers or the Beatles or the Partridge Family, not that I would ever listen to that bubble gum stuff. I have no idea how I still know all of the words to "I Think I Love You." NO, it has nothing to do with that cute little girl in my third grade class who told me that was her favorite song.

Murphy's was also the place where I spent most of my money on toys. It was a vast selection of three twenty foot long aisles filled with Barrels of Monkeys and Klackers and Duncan Yo-Yos. It was also one of the few places I have ever known where it cost a dime to use the restroom. Now if that ain't uptown then I don't know what is! The best part of the experience however, was the snack counter. My dad and I always got the same thing. The best thing there was a bag of warm roasted cashews. They were so rich and creamy, just a taste of heaven. I would give just about anything to walk into G.C. Murphy's one more time with my dad just to look around while sharing a bag of those warm nuts on a cold winter's day.

My First New Car

Many things in my life have been quite unique experiences compared to most individuals. This is certainly true of my first new car buying experience. I was 18 and working and playing music and living with my parents and I felt that I was ready for a brand new ride. I knew very little about the car industry, but I was young and bold and just jumped right into looking. It was not long before I found a nice little number at the American Motors Dealership. I told the sales guy that this was the car I wanted to buy. He asked me about a co-signer. I said I did not have one. I wanted to buy this car by myself. He looked at me doubtfully. I told him I wanted to finance it through the loan company up the street. He asked me with great reservation if I had been pre-approved. I said no. It then took about three requests but finally he gave into my suggestion of calling the finance company to see what I needed to do. You could tell that he thought this was a waste of time.

It was a picture worth a thousand words to witness what happened next.

He said, "This is John from AMC and I have a young gentleman here who wants to finance a new car."

The person on the other end of the line said, " What is his name?"

The sales guy replied, "Lynn Hewitt."

The person then replied, "He's approved. Go ahead and write it up."

The sales guy nearly passed out right there.

What had happened was that the manager of the finance company was from the same little village as I was from. He knew all of my family and I knew all of his. He was the sort of guy who did business the old fashioned way with a handshake and a promise. He knew that I would be good for the money or that my parents would beat me to death. That was enough collateral for him. I made all of my payments and never made him regret taking that chance on me. Most of all, I just mourn the fact that more business is not conducted in this manner.

The Fairest of the Fairs

Yesterday was the first day of the fair. Not just ANY fair, but THE fair. It is the fair I could not wait to go to every year as a kid. It was a long tradition in a very small village which sat right up the road from my own. I thought it was the grandest place in the whole world! There were rides and games and pretty girls from all over the area. They had tractor pulls and horse pulls and entertainment of all sorts.

I used to ride every ride and many of them twice. I would also try to win stuffed animals at the stand where the rat would run into various colored holes. I also would win my mother a whole new set of fine china every year pitching dimes. This vendor was set up with all sorts of plates and bowls and glasses and basically, if your dime landed in it, you won it. My mother had the most eclectic collection of dishes around!

In my teen years, I started to become a part of the entertainment at the fair. I was in the school band which marched in the parade and I was also in local bands which played music in the grandstand. One year we even got to perform with the Flying Walendas. That was big stuff! Oh, and one time we accidentally caught on fire a cardboard outhouse being used as a prop in our show. That was a big hit with the audience.

Unfortunately, I have rarely had the opportunity to attend the fair over my adult years. It is often hard to get away and travel home for it. I did, however, get the opportunity to do so about 5 years ago. I was saddened and shocked to see how many of the things I had loved had disappeared. The rides were mostly gone as were many of the game booths, lured away by bigger, more profitable venues I suppose. It was good to see that people had adapted and were making their own fun in other ways. They had a talent show and a karaoke contest and a mud bog for locals and their trucks.

Also, unfortunately for me, the mud bog had a special event where you and a partner could participate in a foot race through the mud for a cash prize. You had to hold hands with your partner the whole time. Elizabeth thought it was a great idea to sign me up with her to participate. The mud was thick and sticky and DEEP. At one point during the race, Elizabeth ended up about waist deep in the stuff and stuck like glue. It took all of my energy just to free her from the gooey, gloppy mess. I should have just left her there overnight for talking me into this mess. Even when the event was over, I still had fifty pounds of mud caked to my body.

Even though I will not be attending the fair this year, I will be there in spirit. But, if you get to go to your local fair, have a hot sausage sandwich and a funnel cake for me.

Hairball

Last night I got a bellyache in the middle of the night. I had to go to the bathroom on four separate occasions. On the second trip, I decided to just head for the living room sofa and watch a little TV while I awaited the next attack. I was settled in for no more than a minute when the first cat arrived. Cats are always up for sharing a good nap. They think that is what couches are for. Cat number two joined the party about five minutes later and a third quickly followed. It was now a purring and kneading frenzy. They were quite annoyed when I had to get back up and run down the hallway, but they quickly settled back in upon my return. All was forgiven. All in all it was pretty cool. They let me control the remote and they allowed me to pet them. By this morning my stomach was feeling better and all was back to normal. I think I may have just had a hairball or something.

Old Dog

Three weeks ago yesterday I had to take our old dog to the vet. She is approximately 14 and she was really looking to be in dire straits. I truly thought she was gonna die any second. She was not eating. She was lethargic. She had no desire to even raise her head.

The vet said she was showing signs of liver failure and possibly cancer. Her suggestion was that I have the old dog put to sleep. I told her I wanted to take a wait and see approach and asked what we could do to support her and make her comfortable. So, they gave her a steroid injection and injected two big humps of fluid into her back. The dog looked like a camel.

I brought her home and pretty much forced her to eat a little canned food at a time. She had diarrhea and vomiting and just looked miserable. After a couple of days, she began to show minor improvement. She would eat a little on her own and the vomiting had subsided. I figured it was just the steroids and that I had merely bought the old dog a few extra days for the kids to say goodbye.

The trouble with that theory is that she showed more improvement every single day. More interest, more appetite, more energy. I began to actually have a smidgen of hope for her. Day after day, Fluffy was coming back.

So, here we are 22 days after what could have been her last, and the old dog is better than she has been in a year. The family is amazed. The vet is amazed. Fluffy is just loving all of the attention and the canned dog food she is receiving. She is now running around and involved and acting like her old self again. She is off the steroids and antibiotics and all she is taking is the dog equivalent of a Geritol tablet.

I know her time will come and it could come at any time, but for the moment, she looks like she may have fooled us all and may actually be around for quite some time to come. I am glad I did not give up on her 22 days ago.

Al Ironed Out

Sally goes to the hospital today for an iron infusion. Her hemoglobin has always run low, but recently, it seemed to fall even further. Sally is an active girl and very stubborn, so aside from feeling tired and a bit short of breath, she has not allowed this to stop her from doing her daily routine … you know, bossing me around, assigning me chores, criticizing my choices of coordinating pants and shirts etc. …

This is actually Sally's second iron infusion in a week. The first one was a true adventure. They started off by giving her a small test dose via IV and then waited an hour to look for any adverse reaction. All went smoothly. At the end of the hour, Sally told the nurse that the only thing she was feeling was a mild case of heartburn. Hardly cause for alarm considering we had eaten lunch during the test dose.

So, next they came in with this big bag of black fluid and connected it to Sally's IV. She was to receive 1500 units of the stuff over a period of 4 hours. Sally and I played cards for a few minutes and all was well. I began to feel my lunch working on me, so I retired to the private restroom for a little siesta.

I had been in there about 5 minutes when I heard the nurse in the room talking to Sally. I could not hear what was being said, but I assumed she was just checking in on her. Shortly thereafter, I heard another nurse join in the conversation and there seemed to be a lot of activity going on out there. Equipment was being moved around and such. I was curious what the heck could be going on.

I hastily finished my business and exited the siesta room to find Sally being connected to an EKG with two concerned nurses standing there. Sally had a distressed look on her face. She had called the nurse shortly after I had left because she had suddenly felt flushed and her chest felt heavy. The oddest physical appearance was that her ears were now bright red and she complained that they itched terribly. Sally was having a severe allergic reaction to the infusion.

The infusion was quickly terminated and Sally was loaded up on medications to combat the reaction. This made Sally quite sleepy and she spent the afternoon napping at the hospital. In the end, Sally itched in various places for a few days but eventually it all wore off. I offered on various occasions to help her scratch but she just gave me a stern look.

Today they will try a slightly different version of the medicine and see how Sally reacts to a small test dose. I will remain at the ready to help scratch if needed.

Swim

I can't swim! There, I said it. It is all my brother Charles' fault. When he was maybe 15, he went to a big creek with a bunch of other kids and fell into a deep hole in the water and nearly drowned. Therefore, my mom would not let me go within fifty yards of a pool.

After years of avoidance, I finally decided to take the plunge and try to learn along with my kids when they wanted to learn. The four of us went to the YMCA for so many weeks of lessons. The instructor made great progress with the 3 kids, but she seemed to avoid me like I was some sort of hideous monster. She would yell "keep those floaties on" in my direction at the kiddie pool while she was over in the deep end with my little charges. Since then, a few others have tried with limited success. They all say they don't understand why I sink so much. I try to explain to them that it is because I am made of solid muscle, but for some reason they just give me a funny look. Also, I can swim a wee little bit using just my arms in shallow water where I can stand up, but when they try to tell me to kick my feet it doesn't help. People will put a flotation device under my arms and tell me to kick, but when I do that I become the only human in existence who can swim backward. Yes, you should see the looks on their faces when I start actually moving in reverse by kicking. At this point my teacher will quickly view me as a lost cause and silently swim away.

So, while I truly wish I could swim like everyone else, I may always remain the old guy who simply smiles and waves from the shallow end of the pool.

Planning Project

Most days I wake up with a plan, an idea of what I want to get accomplished today. I usually have wonderful intentions. The results? Well, let's just say I often get a bit sidetracked. Today my plan is to work on the Mancave (2 car garage that never sees a car). Ever since the yard sale a few weeks ago, the mancave has been in a state of disorder. Sally says that it is always in a state of disorder, but she simply fails to understand the complexities of my organizational systems. Also, the fact that she tries to unload all of her junk that has no home by throwing it into the Mancave does not help matters. Therefore, today I plan to go out and get things back under control. I will get the tools where the tools go and the fun stuff where the fun stuff goes and Sally's junk to the corner out of my way and so on. Of course, I may get distracted by other "sub-projects" that I come across that need my attention and I am certain Sally will come interrupt my important work with something she deems more important to do, like mow the grass or paint the house. In the end, I once again am starting my day with the best intentions. So, off I go to … well, to first have lunch. Yes actually my day started a while ago. I had a brief appointment to attend and then I stopped by the pet store for food and treats. But, right after lunch I intend to jump right on the important work of reorganizing the Mancave. Well, I do need to run to the post office to mail that one package so maybe I will do that right after lunch. Do the Cubs play on T.V. this afternoon? I need to check that too.

Doctor Bill

I got a bill in the mail yesterday. Well, actually it was a statement. A bold statement if you ask me. It was from my neurologist (by the way I am feeling great for those of you who may be wondering). The neurologist has done in his office about 4 different tests. An EEG (brain scan), and ENG (nerve check via electrocution), actually he did like 2 versions of each of those tests and then he gave me an injection. The total amount billed … $7800.00

The injection of steroids and anti-inflammatory drug was over $400 and that took 10 seconds. Let's see, if we had the patients all lined up and ready … let's be generous here and give him 30 seconds per injection … you know a rest period between them … that's 2 per minute or 120 per hour at $400 each = $48000.00 per hour. Either that medicine is VERY expensive or somebody is getting VERY rich. Ok, so yes he took a minute to talk to me and he did have to write on a chart. Come to think of it he did go on vacation the next week …

Jello Blues

I was talking with my good friend yesterday about an upcoming cookout that they were hosting. In conversation, they mentioned that they were having Jell-O for dessert. I love Jell-O. But that is where the story becomes more complicated.

Yes, I love Jell-O. Yet, as a child, I was tormented by a mother who was determined to fill my Jell-O with stuff that was good for me. She seemed to have a thing against plain Jell-O! It somehow scarred me for life! My demented mother would fill my Jell-O with pineapples or bananas or strawberries. TAKE THOSE STRAWBERRIES AND GO MAKE A PIE MOM AND LEAVE MY DAMNED JELLO ALONE! Oh, um sorry, I may have a small bit of pent up anger about this subject.

But then of course there was the worst one of all. The nearly unspeakable Jell-O atrocity. Dare I even say it? The CARROT JELLO! When mom would fill my Jell-O with fruit, I could pick around it over the next few hours and get a few good morsels of plain Jell-O. However, when she devised her sinister plan to fill my Jell-O with shredded carrots, there was now no place to hide.

She was truly an evil woman! I think she was trying to get back at me for all of that diaper changing or something.

Anyhow, as I was saying, I was talking to my friend and I suddenly had this craving for either green or orange Jell-O. That's right, plain Jell-O filled with , well, Jell-O. You hear that mom! So, I decided to stop by the store and pick up one of those pre-made Jell-O six packs they now sell. I was absolutely amazed and elated that they now have a six pack that is three green and three orange! I was in heaven. Tonight I would satisfy both of my Jell-O cravings! And tomorrow? That is the day I would call mom and rub it in! I ate Jell-O without stuffing and I liked it!

You now know how thinking gets me into trouble. Well, writing this story was the start of me having a craving for non-chunky, unstuffed Jell-O. So I stopped by the grocery store and picked up a six pack on the way home. It was the perfect plan. I pulled out one of the little cups and headed off to the Mancave to hide out and enjoy the first of my six little treasures. It was great! I was in for a fabulous evening of Jell-O bliss.

About twenty minutes later I returned to the fridge for my second helping. Much to my horror I discovered nothing but an empty cardboard Jell-O package! I felt so violated, so deprived! One of the sweet little heathens running around this house had discovered my stash and to make it worse, they then told all of the other little heathens about it too! Such is life in a house of seven kids. Well, six kids and Sally. The other is in his junior year in college and is rarely home. Good thing, because all he ever does is raid my stash of cashews!

Kids make everything expensive. If I am driving down the street and decide to pull in the gas station for a Coke, that drink should cost me about $1.25 these days, but when you have six kids in the car that same drink costs me $8.75. For some reason they seem to think that they are all thirsty at the same time too. And if I am not careful, that $1.25 Coke will end up costing closer to $20 because not only are the kids thirsty, but all of the sudden they are starving as well and by the time they get Slim Jims and Skittles and Snickers and Gummy Worms, I can kiss that $20 goodbye.

I would be rich if not for those little tormentors of mine! I would have money to burn. But the truth is that I would also be poor in many much more important ways. So, I will just have to do better at hiding my Jell-O from now on and go on enjoying all of the great things my children do for my life.

―

To the tune of the old Christmas song, this is what I will be singing to my children early tomorrow morning as I have for many years now on that glorious day in August when school begins …

It's the hap, happiest time of the year!

The school bus is coming and kids will be running the hell out of here!

It's the hap, happiest time of the year!

The end

Seven hours of peace and quiet will soon be returning to my home!

Yeehaw! Yippee! Hooray!

Mystery of Life

    Life is just full of mysteries. There are an incredible number of things that we simply accept without really understanding, things we simply know will occur. Like, I rarely think twice about whether or not gravity will all of the sudden stop working. I am sure that there are people out there who fully understand how gravity works, however I am not one of them. I just expect it to continue doing its thing. Also, without fail, I can count on our two dogs to be happy to see me. They are always wagging their tails and stuff when I come in the door. They are probably just hopeful that I stopped by the pet store for treats, but nonetheless they seem happy to see me. I can also always count on Sally to offer to either text or drive for me every single time I try to do both when she is in the car. If only she could follow herself down the road one day as she drives, texts, talks on the phone and signs to the deaf kids. You would swear she had just come out of Bob's bar and grill a few blocks back. I can count on each of the kids to need something every time we set foot inside a store. All of the sudden there is something they simply cannot do without. I can usually count on the drive-thru to miss one thing on my order.

You get home one bag short on cinnamon twists and there is hell to pay. I also can count on the mailman to be running late when I am anxiously awaiting an important package. I can count on my 17 yr old's car to break down weekly. She is on a first name basis with everyone at the tow truck company.

These and a thousand more things help to make my life what it is. Isn't it great to know that there are so many things you can count on in this world?

Today is move back to college day. Pack up all of my kid's stuff and kinda slow down as I drive past their dorm and shove them out. No sense in that sappy notion of going inside and helping them decorate and organize. They will have it all a mess in a week anyways. Besides who will miss them at home? More food for me at the dinner table right? One less rugrat fighting me for the television remote.

We currently have two in college. Next year it will be three. The house is beginning to feel a little empty. Only five kids remaining. It is kind of like a countdown to old age. 4 kids left, 3 kids left, 2 kids left, 1 kid left, throw mom and dad in the nursing home! Actually, they will probably just slow down as they drive by and shove me out the door.

That's My Girl

Shelly called from college this morning. Her roommate had arrived and moved in. Shelly was raised by me, a guy, so she knows how to do things like a guy. Her roommate is much more girly. For instance, her roommate arrived with a shoe rack with 22 pairs of shoes all neatly organized, her clothes all on hangers, an iron, drawer organizers and was talking about how she needed an umbrella rack. Shelly owns 3 pairs of shoes, crammed her clothes into the dresser drawers, has never used an iron in her life (if something is just too wrinkly, I taught her to go throw it in the dryer for 5 minutes), and she does not own an umbrella. Her roommate asked what she does when it rains and Shelly responded, "I run!" Yep! That's my girl!

Stories

I want to write about the man I know who is probably in his early seventies, but looks like he is about 143. Of course he looked that same way 30 years ago. I also want to write about when I used to play music and all of the characters I encountered. There are stories in me about how I am fascinated with the old woman who works as a greeter at a local department store. She is so cheerful that you just want to beat her up! Well, ok, not really, but I have never seen someone so happy and animated like a cartoon character. I was once in a tornado. That would make a good story. Or maybe the time Curt and I jacked up the car and put it in reverse to see if the miles would go off the odometer. We had a motive for wanting that to work ... well, first we actually tried driving backward but that was not an easy task either. Maybe I should do a story about pool mulching. Yes, black mulch and pools do not mix. I have stories about things like money blowing across a frozen parking lot which was found by a hungry college student and stories about a man who woke up one morning after drinking too much in a city a few hundred miles from home with cash in his pocket and two bullets missing from a gun. He had no clue how any of this happened. I want to write about outhouses and buckets on stairs when the outhouse was too cold. There is also the car I sold to someone who wrecked it and totaled it 3 miles later. Or how about the wallet I found in a KFC restroom and the good feeling of witnessing its return to its rightful owner who had no idea I was the one who had found it. I could go on and on. Happy sad, funny, impossible to believe. I've found my calling in telling my stories.

Spoiled Plans

I have been anticipating today for 3 months now. Today is the first day where all of the kids are to be in school and I have nothing in particular planned in my nice, quiet house. I have been awaiting this moment all summer. However, I awoke this morning to learn that one of the little darlings is sick. I will not mention which little monster ruined my perfect plan with a 102 degree fever. Why can't they go to school with a fever anyhow? If they stay home they are just gonna sneeze and cough all over me and make me sick! And so now I have been transformed from bachelor for a day into Mr. Nursemaid Mom. And next we get to go to the doctor's office where all the sick little kids are!.

Gardens

My vegetable garden has gone to pot. We have had so many hot, dry days this month with temps well up in the 90's that my watermelons and cantaloupes and pumpkins have simply given up trying. Then, the tomatoes are a whole nuther story. Something keeps eating the green tomatoes off of the plant when they get about as big as a golf ball. It must be the deer. That is the only animal I might suspect of doing that. I was having several cucumbers for awhile, but they have slowed down as well and the raccoons enjoyed the corn before I ever got the chance. I had envisioned the garden providing a bountiful harvest for me, but it seems that the wild critters are the ones who enjoyed the fruits of my labor. I am left with the alternative of going to the farmer's market and paying someone else for my garden goods. That is ok too. I rather enjoy the trip.

I have never been great at gardening like my parents. Of course I approach it differently. My parents would be up at the crack of dawn about twice a month with hoe in hand doing battle with the weeds. I am more of a "let the strongest survive" kind of gardener. I look at yard work the same way. And let me tell you, it works!

I have the healthiest dandelion population in my neighborhood every spring. Everyone else has drab green yards while mine is awash in a sea of yellow.

I think I just need to adjust my eating habits rather than fight with mother nature over which plants will survive. Does anyone out there have a good recipe for crabgrass stew? How about thistle salad?

It would have a certain "kick" to it, right? I gotta get busy. I see a bestselling, eco-friendly cookbook in my future!

Potty Procedures

I am here to discuss the bathroom. I suffer at the hands of five women with whom I attempt to share this space. They do not play fair! I go to the store about once every three months and buy 6 hairbrushes. I place them in the hairbrush drawer in the bathroom. These brushes disappear at a rate of about 1 per week never to be seen again. Where do they go? Somebody has to have them. Do hairbrushes magically appear in the bathrooms of other people's homes? Somebody out there must have a crapload of them! I wish they would return like two or three hundred of them to me!

Next is the toilet paper. When I was a bachelor, a roll would last 3 to 4 weeks. In my house full of women, the roll maybe lasts a day. What's up with that? Are they eating the stuff? I mean how many sheets does it take? How many trees must be harvested to keep these women fresh and tidy?

Finally, MY razor. That's right I said MY razor. These women can have fourteen other razors around the house and they will use them up or lose them. They always come back to MY razor. MY razor is for shaving faces, not for harvesting a tropical forest from your legs! Also, it is not necessary to put in a new blade every time you use it. Your legs ain't that pretty! And when I do run out of blades, it is ok for you to pick some up at the store. And don't act like you don't know what the package looks like. You had no trouble identifying it when you found it hidden in my sock drawer. Besides, think of poor me trying to shave with a dull blade. It would be less painful to simply pluck out those whiskers with a pair of tweezers!

A Charlie Brown World

As you may or may not know, I wear hearing aids. I am not deaf, but I do have about a 60% hearing loss in both ears. It is partially attributed to playing music in bands for much of my life. Loud amplifiers, loud drums, a few off key singers … not me, of course. In layman's terms, without my hearing aids I often hear the sounds around me, but just not as clearly as most people do. Without my hearing aids people's voices resemble the adults in a Charlie Brown movie. I hear the noise but cannot distinguish the words. Actually, I get every third or fourth word and then have to fill in the blanks on my own. This can lead to some awkward interpretations.

They might say " Sir your credit card is no good. Do you want to wash dishes?

I might hear "Sir, wah credit wah wah wah good. wah wah want wah wah dishes?"

To which I might answer, "Sure! Give me a setting for four!"

They also might say, "I'm looking for the fastest way to get back on the interstate. Would you be so kind as to direct me?"

I might hear, "I'm wah wah wah fastest wah wah wah back wah wah wah. Would wah wah wah kind wah wah wah me?"

To which I might answer, "Yes, I agree."

Needless to say, on days when I forget to put in my hearing aids, I do indeed live in a Charlie Brown world. I get odd stares and funny responses all day long. It is easy to mistake one word for another and get a whole new meaning.

I don't complain about my hearing loss. I could have many worse things wrong with me. It is just who I am and I accept that. I guess the most important thing I can say about the whole matter is Wah wah wah wah wah wah. And you can quote me on that.

The Stick Bug Theory

Religion and spirituality are very touchy subjects for us humans. We get very polarized by our beliefs and we tend to be very defensive about them as well. I like to quote the saying I once saw on a poster in a sub shop. It read something to the effect "Have you ever noticed that the man who is eager to share his religious beliefs with you is rarely interested in hearing yours?" It is so true! Many people seem to have the opinion that their views are the only ones that matter on this subject and that everyone else needs to just fall in line. Also, the ones who are the most concrete in their beliefs are often the same ones who are the most outspoken. What ever happened to judge not lest ye be judged?

If you begin to examine religion and begin to look at why various individuals believe as they do, one of the first observations you will be able to make is that most people simply belong to the same faith as their parents did even down to the specific denomination within a particular faith. I find that fact to be quite intriguing. Of course it is not always true, but the percentage of people who are of the same faith as their parents is a very high number. I also find that many people truly know very little about the beliefs of religions other than their own. I also find this fact fascinating.

As for me, I have struggled my whole life with this subject. I have tried to gain an understanding of what my existence is all about and where did it even come from, as well as where it might be going. I did not want to be one of those people who lies to even themself about what they believe. I have sought answers that I can live with. Answers that make sense to me. I do not have it all figured out, but this is kinda where I stand after approximately 50 years of soul-searching.

The first thing that I have concluded is that I am miniscule. Science tells me that my galaxy is like a grain of sand amongst all of the other galaxies out there. When I then consider how small the Earth is in comparison to our galaxy and then in turn how small I am in relation to the Earth, I am a speck!

The second thing that I have concluded is that I am highly complex. I am made up of more stuff than I can count. I have billions of cells in me and they do all sorts of amazing things for me without me even knowing. That makes me a pretty awesome piece of engineering.

The third thing that I have concluded is that I am not capable of comprehending the fullness of this existence. My mind simply cannot grasp all that is going on around me on both a grand and microscopic scale. Take time, for instance. Time is the most valuable thing in the universe from my point of view. It is something you cannot buy, sell, barter or trade. It is absolutely priceless. Did time have a beginning? Does time have an end? My mind cannot fathom either answer to those questions. Beginning? Yes, but what happened before then? What caused it to begin? Beginning? No, well it had to start somewhere! See, for me my mind cannot comprehend those answers. There may be people of greater minds than mine who have this all figured out, but they have not cc'd me the condensed version yet.

So, here I sit. From my perspective I am alive and doing quite well. But why and to what end?

Over the years I have searched various places for answers. I have found that my most reliable answers exist in nature. In nature I find things which I believe are unmanipulated by man and therefore I can trust. For me it is a better source than some other human telling me that this is what I should believe.

Phasmida. That is a big fancy scientific word for the Order that classifies stick bugs. For me, those bugs that look exactly like a stick are a very significant clue to my existence. How the heck did these guys end up looking just like a stick? Was it by natural selection? By chance? Was there an intelligent designer involved? Each human should have the right to answer those questions for themselves without ridicule or wrath from any other human. Next look at a butterfly. Look at the stages of life involved for this critter. It is an amazing feat! Again, I raise the same questions. Gravity. How lucky we are that it just happens to exist. We take it for granted. Male and female. This one I am sure someone can explain, but for me and my little mind to understand how we ended up with two genders that need one another is pretty amazing stuff. I know there are some species who reproduce on their own, but for many that is simply not the case. And how did the berry plant figure out that if it had edible seeds, that some animal would come along and eat those seeds and then later deposit them on down the trail somewhere therefore making more berry plants? These are the things that catch my attention.

We live in such a man made world with our houses and cars and computers, but for me the answers to life tend to lie in nature itself. I find no fault with any religions of the world. There are both good and bad people in all faiths. But for me, I have come to the conclusion that something far beyond my comprehension had a hand in creating me and all that surrounds me. Where it came from? I have no idea. Will it grant me an afterlife? I sure hope so, but again, I have no clue. Those are questions I am still working on. Life is a funny thing. A great mystery to unravel. All I know is that I am truly enjoying the journey.

Hands From Heaven

I have been making trips to the chiropractor over the past couple of months. It has been very beneficial to me. I actually look forward to the visits. The office that I go to utilizes the services of a handful of massage therapists as well who get you all loosened up before the doctor works you over. One therapist in particular is blessed with what I like to refer to as "Hands from Heaven." She has this way of simply making you melt into the table. I had even commented to my wife Sally that if this woman were to ask me to marry her during one of my massages, I would probably say yes.

As fate would have it, Sally recently developed a "kink" in her own back. She had never been to a chiropractor, but decided that the pain had become so unbearable that she was willing to give it a try. I was curious to see how she would respond to this sort of treatment. I was not sure if she would like the experience. I soon got my answer with her brief commentary when she returned home that day from her first appointment.

She said simply, "You can't marry that woman you like at the chiropractor's office, because I am going to."

My Helper

I had been looking forward to a day of rest and relaxation for quite some time. I had it all planned. No plans at all. Just a day to goof off and do a whole lot of nothing. So, the night before my day of relaxation, Sally called me on my cell phone and informed me that the kitchen sink was clogged. Being the nice guy that I am, I told her that I would take care of it in the morning. I also made the mistake of letting her know that I had nothing at all planned for the following day.

The next morning I arose expecting to do a quick fix on the sink and then get on with my big day of nothing. The trouble was that Sally had already planned my day out for me. That's what I get for letting her in on my plan. She had decided it was time to clean, reorganize and redo the entire basement. This whole plan involved me moving things, rewiring things, fixing things, cleaning things. It was horrible!

On top of all of this, the sink turned into a much bigger job than I had anticipated. The line coming from the sink, disposal and dishwasher was completely clogged. At the far end of the house is an access point in this line for cleanout. I opened this pipe but got nothing out except for a strong, ugly stench. This was when I got my just reward. I told Sally that I was gonna have to go up to the other end of the drain and try to unplug the clog with a plumbing snake. Her job was to hold a bucket under the open line in case it began to drain. Long story short, Sally did not listen very well and ended up with a face full of rotted food, grease and who knows what else. She was not a happy camper. I was highly entertained. It kinda made the whole day worthwhile.

———

Am I the only one who finds life tremendously humorous? Today I was driving out of the parking lot of a strip mall when I noticed a woman who was standing in the doorway of a store. It was a GNC vitamin store. The sign above her head said GNC Live Well. She was standing there propping open the door with her foot with a phone held to her ear, wearing her GNC uniform, and smoking a cigarette. So this is the woman who is gonna show me how to live a healthier life? I sure wish I had taken a picture.

Take That, Sparky

I was recently having a conversation with a good friend when the subject of books came up. This "friend" has said that they enjoyed my stories and that I "crack them up." Yet when this "friend" and I started talking books they were awfully quick to blurt out, "My favorite author is Sparks."

Their true colors came quickly shining through! I was like "Hey! What about me!" They quickly came up with some concocted story about how I was their favorite funny short story author from the specific side of the street where I grew up, but I could tell that old Sparky was winning this battle. What did this guy have that I didn't have besides millions of readers and the fact that he writes mushy chick books.

Oh well, what's a guy to do? I know! I will write my own mushy chick book. Let's see! How should I begin …

Eduardo's muscles rippled beneath the sweat of his bare naked chest as he labored beneath the baking sun. His long locks of golden hair were hanging limply … you see, the drug store had been out of stock on his favorite conditioner. But now was not the time to worry about limp hair. The chicken coop had to be cleaned today and he was over halfway done. Just fifty more pounds of chicken poop to be removed and he would be able to return home to his trophy wife, Ethel.

Take that Sparky! So what do you think? A new avenue for my career is born? A bestseller in the making?

Forms

Sometimes life can be a pain in the neck, but then again that is a little too obvious. Things do not always go smoothly with everything we try in this life. I had just such an experience today. An organization I am working with needed some documents from me. You know, the kind of documents that I will spend half a day getting together so that they can be stuffed in a file where nobody will ever look at them again. It's silly really. So, in this modern age, some of these documents are only available online. Many companies have simply stopped mailing out stuff to save money. Anyhow, I went online and found this information, but when I go to print, behold the printer is out of ink again! So, off to the store I go … not the first store which was out of stock on my ink … not the second store which no longer carries my ink … aha! finally, the third store had it in stock for a premium ransom. Back home I go, ink in hand!

I get home, install the ink cartridge and click the button to connect to the internet … nothing. The internet service was now down! Are you kidding me? After three phone calls lasting approximately four and a half days, my service was restored. So I now have these useless pieces of paper in hand and it only took me all day to gather them. Like I said, a pain in the neck, my friend.

The other day I was talking with an elderly gentleman and at the end of our conversation I told him to have a great day. He responded by saying that every day is a great day. He flashed a big smile and went on his merry way. I got to thinking. We always look forward to the next holiday or next season or event. These days are all special because we have chosen to make them so. In honesty, every single day should be cherished and not simply wished away or tolerated. If you choose to make every day a special day, your life will be much more fulfilling and rewarding. That one brief comment from that old man has got me thinking that I need to work more on cherishing each and every day and a lot less complaining.

Fire In the Hole

The other day my sinuses were a bit stuffy and I was hungry too. I decided to resolve both issues by stopping by a little Cajun joint that I have visited in the past for a big helping of Jambalaya. This place serves it up with garlic toast and plenty of heat. It is not the kind of spicy heat that makes your tongue burn, but instead, it is the kind that makes your eyeballs sweat. It is great for cleaning out the sinuses.

Anyhow, that particular day's offering was even hotter than usual. It not only cleaned my sinuses and made my ears sweat but also relieved me of a few extra brain cells up in there somewhere. I know that there are those who would say I have no brain cells to spare, but that is a whole 'nuther story. I just know that I left the place quite proud of myself for curing my hunger and my sinus problem all at once. Until 3 hours later that is ... That is when I was finding myself in need of some little chalky pills to cure the burning in my belly. The fire kept building and I kept throwing little pills at it. After about 90 minutes that fire seemed to subside and was quickly forgotten. Until that evening about an hour after dinner when the fires of Hell decided it was time to vacate my body! Oh My God! How does something get 150 times hotter in a 3 foot trip? I felt like I was being subjected to torture with a blowtorch! Indeed I had cleaned out my sinuses, but next time I will think twice before curing it with Jambalaya.

Sneeze

Sneeze. Go ahead, sneeze, right now. You can't do it! I know I may be a bit goofy, but I am fascinated by things we often take for granted. We cannot sneeze at will without some sort of trigger like ground black pepper or pollen or dust. Why is that? A sneeze is such a violent rush of air and it sure does have a good purpose. It also feels good to sneeze. So why do we have very little control over it? I know, just the ponderings of a lunatic here.

My wife, Sally, is the weird one. When she feels the need to sneeze, she runs outside and looks for the sun. She claims that looking at the sun makes her sneeze. Now, what is that all about? And they call me crazy! I have witnessed her do it. It actually seems to work. I have no idea why. I must admit that I have tried this method and it does nothing for me.

Allergies cause people to sneeze a lot. I know I seem to sneeze more in the Fall because of the stuff in the air. Not all allergies make me sneeze. For instance, Sally says I am allergic to chores, but they do not make me sneeze.

Smelling Dinner

I am excited. It is chilly outside and Sally made stew with cornbread! Ain't that the life! I can smell it simmering right now. There is not much better than cornbread. I can eat it with just about anything. I will settle down after dinner to either read the newspaper or watch a little TV and just relax. Then Sally will come into the room and say, "Just who do you think you are? I made dinner now you do the dishes!"

Then she will bring up the fact that the laundry needs folding and the cat litter needs changing and … Oh well, at least I can enjoy my stew until then.

Sharing My Knowledge

All of us learn many things over the course of our lives. By the time we are old and gray, we hopefully have a lot of wisdom. I believe that it is important to share that wisdom with the future generations so that they can learn from it and expand upon it and grow to possess even greater knowledge. So, today I am here to impart some of my own personal wisdom upon you.

I have come to know many things over the course of my fifty-plus years on this Earth. I can never hope to share all of what I know in one book, but hopefully each of you can learn from my experiences.

For instance, I have learned that if you have children in the house and you bring home a special treat for yourself from the grocery store which you are planning to consume while watching the football game on TV tomorrow, forget it! No matter how well you hide it, they will find it and eat it before you ever get the chance. I have also learned that if your wife sounds annoyed when asking you again when you are gonna fix that leaking toilet, it is best to speak gibberish and then act like you just received an important call on your cell phone, which of course was on vibrate, which is why she did not hear it ring. This tactic actually works well for many jobs she may have for you.

I have also learned that when your wife says that you need to help do things around the house, she will not be satisfied if you just take it upon yourself to just do stuff without checking with her first. You will quickly find that the stuff you find that needs doing was not on her list at all! She will fail to see the importance of the entertainment system being able to record two sports shows at the same time, she just wants all of those damned wires hidden.

I have also learned that if the mailman is bringing nothing but bills, he will arrive at 9am, but if you are waiting on a big check and you are broke, he will show up exactly one minute after the bank has closed for the day.

I have discovered that raking leaves is silly. It is better to just wait for a windy day. Then they will all blow into your neighbor's yard and he can rake them.

So, there is just a small part of what I have learned. Don't you feel enlightened now?

Diagnosing Myself

I had a birthday last week. It was a great day. I got three pumpkin pies and a pumpkin roll, four new pillows for my bed (the little heathens around this house are always stealing my pillows), some clothes, including a very cool personalized t-shirt, and a new harmonica, amongst other stuff. I ate homemade pizza and watched a football game on TV. All of my kids were there at some point during the day. It was all I could have hoped for and more.

The trouble is that I do not feel nearly as old as I am. Inside this achy, saggy body remains a sixteen year old kid. I often attempt to do the same stuff I did when I was sixteen and then I pay the price when my body betrays me. I used to be able to put my foot behind my head, now it is a struggle to merely reach my foot with my outstretched fingertips. What the heck went wrong along the way? I used to fall down or get tackled or knocked down at some point just about every day. I would simply bounce back up and keep going. Now, when I fall down, I feel as if I need to go crawl into bed for three days and it hurts! I also feel clumsy and awkward. Where the heck did that come from? I feel like somebody came in and stole my body. Of course, I am still as handsome as ever, actually even more so, but for some reason I just can't seem to do the same old tricks as easily as I used to. Maybe I am just not getting enough sleep. That's gotta be it! I am gonna work on getting a good ten hours a night from now on. I bet I will be climbing trees and jumping fences again in no time!

Pushing the Purse

Have you ever noticed that when a man and woman go to the store together that usually it is the man who is pushing the cart around with the woman's purse in it? Often these "purses" more closely resemble suitcases meant for a weekend stay at a resort in terms of size. What the heck do they keep in there anyhow? Do you mean to tell me that this baggage is filled with the stuff she dare not leave the house without? Men keep all of these necessities neatly tucked away in their wallet and their pockets.

Being the curious type, I got brave and peeked into Sally's purse. I am here to tell you that I will have nightmares for weeks to come due to the experience. It makes me wonder what the real Sally must be like once you take away all of those creams and makeups and prescription drugs and shopper's loyal discount cards and toiletries and candy and 14,000 receipts and pictures of her and the mailman on some exotic beach and …

Hey! Wait a minute!

www.ingramcontent.com/pod-product-compliance
Lightning Source LLC
Chambersburg PA
CBHW031641040426
42453CB00006B/177